D0829209

SOCIAL GRAVITY

HARNESSING THE NATURAL LAWS OF RELATIONSHIPS

BY JOE GERSTANDT AND JASON LAURITSEN

TALENT ANARCHY

ISBN-13: 978-061-558-7875

ISBN-10: 0615587879

The greatest compliment you can give an author is to read their book and, if you are moved by it, to share with others. Please refer this book to your friends should you like it.

Not only are Joe and Jason thought-provoking writers, they are wicked good keynote speakers. You should book them for your next conference or event. Your audience will thank you.

You can learn more about the authors and their work at www.TalentAnarchy.com.

Reach Joe Gerstandt at joe@talentanarchy.com.

Reach Jason Lauritsen at jason@talentanarchy.com.

DEDICATION

We humbly dedicate this book to the people in our lives without whom, we would not be who we are today.

To Angie and Gina, our remarkable wives, for their love, support, belief, and most importantly, patience.

To Dylan, Haydn, Gillian, Bailey, Colton, and Oscar, our children, for the daily gift of magic and inspiration that only a child can provide.

To Joan and Steve Lauritsen and Cecilia and Marvin Gerstandt, our parents, for being our role models and giving us permission to believe that we could change the world.

CONTENTS

If you are on the fence about reading this book, scan through the introduction. It's a bit about who we (the authors) are, what Social Gravity is, and how this book can change your life if chose to read it.

The first half of the book is about understanding the what and why of social gravity. It's about the nature of relationships, how networks form and produce value, and what you need to know to embrace how social gravity can transform your life.

...It's Who You Know That Matters

Think who you know doesn't matter? The true importance of who you know and who they know in your personal and professional life will be revealed as we define the concept of social capital. Social capital is the tangible value created when you successfully harness social gravity.

Survey Says: Who You Know Matters, But We Don't Like It

We outline the findings of some original research done by the authors in partnership with Quantum Workplace to explore employee perceptions of the importance of relationships within the workplace, specifically as it relates to getting promoted and getting ahead.

Anatomy of a Network

Malcolm Gladwell. Mark Granovetter. Robin Dunbar. W.L. Gore. That is a lot of name dropping in one chapter. Here we explore the work of these experts to examine how relationships and networks form, including the role of proximity, the difference between strong ties and weak ties, and overlap (the difference between quantity and quality of relationships).

Where the Power Lies

We hold this truth to be self-evident: all connections are not created equal. This chapter builds on the previous one to show the path toward building a powerful network. We all have limited time and resources for building relationships, so it's critical to learn how to wisely invest your time and resources by looking for opportunities to add reach, diversity, and power to your network.

This is Your Network on Technology

I am on Facebook, therefore I am connected, right? Maybe not. Social media doesn't necessarily translate into social capital, but it can be a tremendously powerful tool. The craze over social media can be confusing and daunting. We provide the information you need to make well-informed decisions about what to use, why to use it, and how to leverage social media to harness social gravity to your benefit.

DISCOVER THE LAWS OF SOCIAL GRAVITY

Time to get busy. By this point, you will understand that Social Gravity can transform your life if you learn how to effectively harness it. The second half of this book builds on this foundation by providing the tools you need to unleash the power of social gravity in your life. This will be revealed to you through the Six Laws of Social Gravity.

First Law: Invest in Connecting

The first law takes principles often applied to financial capital and applies them to relationships. Knowing your goals, understanding the power of compounding, and taking the long-term approach are simple yet significant guidelines for being focused and intentional about building a robust network of relationships.

Second Law: Be Open to Connections

It may seem obvious to say that you can't connect to someone if you aren't open to it, but as you will find, it's easier said than done. The second law challenges you to be on the lookout for the many mental barriers inherent in being human that get in the way of making and growing important connections with other people.

Third Law: Be Authentic

Being who you are is the only way to create long-term, authentic relationships. Discover some big and bold approaches like writing a personal manifesto and flying your freak flag! Human beings are social animals and, more specifically, herd animals, so we are wired to try to blend in and hide the things that make us different. Fitting in is dangerous because authenticity is a necessity for harnessing the power of social gravity.

Fourth Law: Get Involved in Meaningful Activity

Networking for the sake of networking doesn't work! It feels contrived because it lacks meaning. Great relationships form from when you are doing something meaningful with others. By finding ways to contribute to efforts that you care about personally and professionally, you will find yourself connected to people that care about the same things that you do. Social gravity at work!

Fifth Law: Use Karma to Turbocharge Your Network

Do good things and good things will happen for you. That's karma. And it is a powerful tool in harnessing social gravity. Simply put, if you have the opportunity to help someone and you are in a position to help without causing harm to yourself, do it. Be generous with people and they will be generous in return.

Sixth Law: Stay in Touch

Growing a powerful network of relationships is like growing a garden. A successful garden requires work and attention. Relationships work the same way. Making connections (planting the seeds) is only part of the equation for establishing the relationships that lead to valuable social capital. In order for connections to become truly valuable, you must stay in touch (tending to the garden). Learn how to do it most effectively.

It's Your Time

It's time to make a decision. Regardless of who you are or where you come from, you can have more social capital tomorrow, if you choose to act now. It is on you, and after reading this book you will have all the tools to make it happen. You do not need a budget, degree, title, or certification. You don't even need to get anybody's permission. You just do it. We do not know how this will play out for you, but we do know how it starts. It starts with you putting the first foot forward.

Survey Questions

Suggested Reading

SOCIAL GRAVITY

INTRODUCTION

Questions can be such powerful things.

Just as sunlight can determine the direction of a plant's growth, questions inform the direction of growth for people and groups of people. Questions attract our attention. They focus our curiosity and inquiry. Questions sharpen our cognitive abilities and reveal our passions. Questions help us to make invisible things visible so that we might understand the world more clearly.

An apple allegedly falls on some guy's head. Rather than cursing the apple or the tree or his bad luck, he asks a powerful question: "Why does the apple fall *down* toward the ground, instead of up toward the sky or to the side? The right question can change everything. It's all so obvious now.

The apple falls down because a force pulls on it. Gravity is one of the fundamental forces that shapes the interactions of all matter in the universe. It

 does not matter that you cannot see it, nor does it matter that it once did not have a name. It doesn't matter whether you agree with it or believe in it. Gravity exists and it is at work on you and the things around you at all times.

Once gravity was "discovered," we were equipped with a deeper understanding of this force governing the interaction of things, having named it and drafted a theory or two on the what, why, and how of it.

This book also began with a question. How do we know so many people? The emergence and growth of our professional network was the symbolic apple that fell on our heads. We wondered how it came to be and why it had happened as it did. This focused our curiosity and passions, and it led to our discovery of "social gravity."

We aspire to share our discovery and to make social gravity visible to you. We will reveal to you the invisible forces that cause people and groups to come together to create value and benefit one another. Social gravity is the force that attracts opportunity, ideas, and information, so that you can be at greater risk of having them land directly on you. Social gravity creates intersections with other people.

This is not a small thing.

Ours is a time of great challenge, complexity, and increasing volatility, and the ability to marshal the resources of a large, dynamic, and robust network is a big part of the way forward. This is part of how we will reimagine how we do community, work, learning, and leadership.

What you know does matter, and it always will. Knowledge and experience have an additive effect on what you have to offer, but your network of relationships can have a multiplicative effect, allowing you to leverage the knowledge and experience of dozens or hundreds or thousands of others to create value and change.

What you know helps you *play* the game, and *who* you know helps you *change* the game.

Social gravity is at work all around you. The question is whether or not you work with it or against it. It's like running up a hill versus running down it. When you run up a hill, your body not only has to do the work of running, but it also has to compensate for gravity pulling you down that hill. Running uphill is hard work. It is tiring and can feel at times like you aren't making a lot of progress. But, running downhill is a very different experience. Running down hill turns the power of gravity into an ally. When running down a hill, it feels as if you run faster and more effortlessly than you ever expected. At times, your path down the hill can almost feel as if it is out of our control, that gravity has taken over all of the hard work.

So, you can fight gravity, or you can let it work for you. Social gravity works in the same way. By understanding it and learning how it works, you can put it to work in powerful ways to fuel your success. This book will provide you with that opportunity. We want you to make an informed choice about what role social gravity will play in your life. Running uphill or downhill is a matter of choice.

Intersections are also powerful.

Intersections are where things of substance crash into each other and sparks are thrown. Unrealized potential exists in intersections.

A student at Harvard named Steve Ballmer meets another student named Bill Gates in a dorm hall. They later become the first two CEOs of Microsoft.

Warren Buffet and Bill Gates meet at a social event in 1991 and the seeds of friendship are sown. As the two richest men in the world, they also go on to partner in challenging the existing idea of philanthropy.

William Procter and James Gamble, one from England and one from Ireland, meet in Cincinnati, Ohio, through the sisters they were dating and would eventually marry. They later form Procter & Gamble, one of the world's largest consumer goods manufacturers.

In early 1999, another such collision took place. It happened in a small business in one of the greatest small cities in America: Omaha, Nebraska. Wandering the professional landscape as well-intentioned malcontents with a desire for more, your authors found themselves working in the same place at the same time. This place we worked was a strange and dysfunctional corner of the business world where we learned much about how not to run a business. Perhaps as a survival instinct or maybe just fueled by curiosity, the two of us struck up a relationship that would ultimately result in a friendship that would span beyond a decade. Our friendship probably could have been predicted. We had some important things in common, among them a hunger to make something happen, to leave our mark on the world. This compulsion mixed with our chronic impatience led the two of us to start a couple not-for-profit organizations shortly after we met, both aimed at creating positive change in our community.

It was through the hard work of building and growing these organizations that the foundational experience underlying the message in this book was gained. Ask anyone who's been involved in community building and you will quickly find out that this kind of work is done with and through people. Communities are made up of people, and it's people that change them. Without the ability to make and sustain great relationships with others, you can't impact your community. These lessons learned in our early days together have proven to be effective in all areas of our lives, so we resolved to share them with you through this book.

Through the years, we have been called a lot of things: trouble makers, rabble rousers, skeptics. But the label we have chosen for ourselves is "talent anarchists." Talent Anarchy is the name that we place on our collaborative work, which is about asking questions and spreading ideas that set talent free. "Anarchy" can be off-putting to some, but that word was carefully chosen. While it brings images of chaos to mind for many people, it means something very different to us. We are not advocates for chaos. We advocate life, choice, and freedom, and we believe that it is often conformity, hierarchy, and cluelessness that stand in the way. Setting talent free is the transformational process of liberating the inner potential locked up or lying dormant inside the organization, the individual, or the relationship. Part of this process is making the invisible visible, which is what we aim to do by illustrating the dynamics of social gravity.

Our messages are deeply rooted in our own experiences. We have always and will always commit ourselves to delivering messages to our audience that are thought provoking, content rich, and intensely practical. Our objective is to help people set talent free—their own and the talent in others.

We see a disheartening amount of talent overlooked, ignored, and wasted. And yet, while most of us get outraged when we see money wasted, we have great tolerance for the squandering of our own talents and the talents of others.

The career woman who works hard and takes her job seriously but watches as her peers get better opportunities because they seem to have an inside connection with management.

The senior executive who is frustrated that it doesn't seem that she can get real information about what's going on in her organization or community.

The young professional who has a great idea for how to improve the community but can't seem to get anyone to listen.

All of these are common examples of wasted talent. Given the right opportunity, each of these individuals could use their talents to do great things. The common thread in these examples is that the path to unleashing this talent is through better relationships with other people. This is what this book is about: putting social gravity to work to unleash your talent and the talent of those around you through the right relationships with other people.

In the following chapters, we will share several stories from our own experiences. We contemplated introducing the stories and experiences of others as well, but it didn't feel authentic. Since much of this has grown directly out of our own adventures, we want to connect our message to its experiential roots.

Some of you will read this book and agree with what we write but never make any real changes. Change requires work; it requires you to start acting differently than you are now. It's scary and it takes abandoning old ideas, beliefs, and behaviors. If you aren't up for it, maybe you should just stop reading now. But, if you are serious about change and are committed to doing what it takes to be wildly successful, for you we have included a section at the end of each chapter titled "Harnessing Social Gravity." In this section you will find activities and exercises that will take the message of this book and make it real for you. In essence, it's your homework. Just like in school, if you do the homework, you are more likely to get great results.

We are also two writers collectively working to craft a single, coherent message. One of the strengths of Talent Anarchy is the blending of two unique perspectives and voices that we bring to the stage and to our writing. To find a happy medium in this book, you will encounter sections labeled "Connected Joe" and "Connected Jason." In these sections, we each share our own stories in our own voices. In this way, we hope that you will benefit from the diversity of our perspectives without being overwhelmed by either one of us. (We even get sick of our own voices sometimes.)

Enjoy the ride.

And please do something with what you find here. Set your talent free.

SOCIAL GRAVITY

Section 1

IT'S NOT <u>WHAT</u> YOU KNOW...

CONNECTED JOE

It was 2006, and I had just gone to work for a large hospital system as its diversity director. After spending my first couple of weeks meeting people and learning my way around, I had some fact finding to do. One of my overarching goals was to make sure that this organization, which was very driven by quality, did a good job of delivering high-quality care to all patients, regardless of race, ethnicity, or any other aspect of their identity. I had seen a fair amount of research showing that racial, ethnic, and gender disparities in healthcare were a significant concern on a national level, and I wanted to make sure that as an organization we were not contributing to these disparities. In a couple of my early meetings with folks that played management, support, or training roles for our workforce of healthcare providers, I mentioned this issue and asked if we looked for these types of disparities on a regular basis. I was given some conflicting information about what data we collected on our patients and how it was collected. Not much help.

So, I did what made sense to me: I pulled up the hospital-system directory on my computer and begin moving through our organizational chart looking for who would be able to clarify this for me. I made several calls. Some of the folks that I spoke to directed me to call other people. Some of the folks that I spoke to just didn't know the answer, and some were confused as

to why I was asking. When I asked one lady involved in patient data about whether race and ethnicity were mandatory fields on our patient intake interface, she whispered to me through the phone, "I don't think it is legal for us to ask that." I love a good challenge, but after playing phone tag with a lot of people and sending and receiving too many emails, I had gotten a little frustrated.

And then a thought occurred to me. I had a good friend that worked for another healthcare organization nearby. He was a well-respected registered nurse and had worked at his organization for several of years. I pulled up his number and made the call. He briefed me on his organization's policy and process for collecting and analyzing patient racial and ethnic data, and he also gave me the phone number of someone at his organization who worked more closely with that issue. She gave me detailed information about their process as well as the historic context for their implementation of this process. More importantly, she gave me the name of the person within my own organization that would be able to help me with the information I needed. Surprisingly, this was a name that nobody within my own organization had given me. And there I was, suddenly feeling the power of social gravity. It took making a call to someone outside of my organzation to get the job done. Had I not made the call to my friend, it may have taken me weeks to find what I was looking for. The old adage "it's not what you know, but who you know" had proven itself once again.

It's one of those phrases we come to know as we grow up: "It's not *what* you know, but *who* you know that really matters." Often, we use these words to explain a situation in which we perceive that an undeserving person came into some sort of reward. A young go-getter gets hired for a job that you feel you should have gotten, for example, and you assume that this person is a family friend of the boss. Or, your neighbor always seems to come up with great seats to major sporting events, while you can never find tickets. So you resent him for it and assume he must be cheating because he has a personal connection.

We seem to have a love-hate relationship with this idea that relationships matter. On one hand, we accept quite easily that things often come to us because of who we know, but on the other hand, when others benefit from their relationships, we think they have taken some sort of shortcut. Some of us even proclaim this as a way of getting something for nothing and proudly declare that we are not going to play that game. "I'm not here to make friends; I am here to do a job!" Sound familiar? Many of us have been taught to uphold a way of thinking that emphasizes respect for the chain of command, paying dues in full, and waiting for fortune to smile upon us. This way of thinking is self-limiting. It holds us back from realizing our potential and achieving all that life has to offer. Opportunity and success run through people and relationships. If you are one of those people who has felt that who you know shouldn't matter, you are standing in your own way. This mindset is similar to driving around town with

> No man is an island entire of itself; every man is a piece of the continent, a part of the main; if a clod be washed away by the sea, Europe is the less, as well as if a promontory were, as well as a manor of thy friends or of thine own were; any man's death diminishes me, because I am involved in mankind. And therefore never send to know for whom the bell tolls; it tolls for thee.
>
> – John Donne

the emergency brake on. You might make progress, but you'll never hit your full potential. It is time to take the brake off. It's time to stop fighting social gravity.

An important disclaimer before we go any further. What you know does matter. Rather than prioritizing "what" you know versus "who" you know, a balanced approach is the best strategy. What you know *and* who you know play different roles in your success, but both are important. Knowledge, competency, experience, poise, curiosity, talent—all of those things are important and valuable. At the same time, your ability to apply those valuable things is dependent upon who you know. The problem, as we see it, is that too often people place all of their faith in what they know to get them ahead, thus ignoring the powerful forces hidden in who they know. It's these hidden forces of social gravity that can make all the difference for you if you chose to embrace and leverage them.

This book represents a different way of thinking about how things work and about your place in the world. It's time to embrace the idea that who you know matters. In fact, who you know makes all the difference when it comes to success in life, love, and work. It's time to realize that in the same way you control what you know, you have a great deal of control over who you know and how you know them. The relationships in your life happen intentionally if you choose to adopt a connection mindset and embrace your relationships with clarity of purpose.

We aim to provide you with an understanding of the power of relationships in your life. We call that power "social gravity." You will learn how the relationships in your life produce a powerful resource called "social capital." As you will discover, social capital is the currency that separates the most successful people on the planet from everyone else. So, if you are currently of the mindset that networking is for chumps, we hope to open your mind in the first section of this book by breaking down some of the science behind social gravity. We'll show you why relationships and connections with other people really matter to the overall quality of your life. If you are already of the mindset that other people are critical to success, this section will give you a deeper understanding of how your connection to other people powers your success. Regardless of where you are starting from, you'll take away some practical approaches and tools to help you find greater success in the future.

To build an understanding of where social gravity comes from and why it is critically important to your success, the chapters in this section will explore the key principles and dynamics at play within the most power networks. Then, in the second section, we will provide you with a practical, "how to" approach to harnessing social gravity so that you can seize all of the success you desire in your life.

Despite what you might expect, this is not another book about networking. We aren't going to share any nifty tips for maximizing a networking event or working a room. We aren't going to talk about power ties, proper handshakes, or clever icebreakers. There are shelves of books already written that can provide you with that type of information. Truth be told, we are not big fans of traditional networking. Instead, we are big fans of authentic, mutually beneficial relationships. The book you are holding is about harnessing the power of connections with other human beings and about how these connections hold the key to personal and professional success.

"A wonderfull harmony arises from joining together the seemingly unconnected."

— Heraclitus

SOCIAL GRAVITY

CHAPTER 1:

...IT'S WHO YOU KNOW THAT MATTERS

Who do you know?

- Who would you call if you lost your job today and needed to find a new one quickly?

- Who do you know that knows where all the best nightclubs are?

- Who can you call if you need a babysitter on short notice?

- Who do you know who can help you fix your lawnmower?

- Who would you call if you needed to find an expert cancer specialist to treat a loved one?

Pretty big questions. Having answers to these questions—answers we feel good about—has significant value to us. We all know that relationships are important. It would be difficult to find anyone arguing that having relationships with other people is a bad thing. It has even been shown that the people you are connected to can play a major role in determining your mood:

> A new study by researchers at Harvard University and the University of California, San Diego, documents how happiness spreads through social networks. They found that when a person becomes happy, a friend living close by has a 25 percent higher chance of becoming happy themselves. A spouse experiences an 8 percent increased chance and for next-door neighbors, it's 34 percent. "Everyday interactions we have with other people are definitely contagious, in terms of happiness," says Nicholas Christakis, a professor at Harvard Medical School and an author of the study.[1]

Not only can your relationships with others impact your mood, they may also affect your health. Research done at Carnegie Mellon University has shown that more-diverse social networks were associated with greater resistance to upper respiratory illness.[2] Holy cow. We can't ignore it. Relationships are really important. But beyond that, this research is telling us not only that it's important to have relationships with others but also that having the *right kinds* of relationships can make all the difference.

This book is not about directly increasing your happiness or health (that will just be a happy by-product of reading it and putting its lessons to work). Rather, this book is about making connections with other people that empower you to make important things happen in life for you and those you care about. It is about pursuing your dreams by putting a powerful tool to work in your life. That tool is social capital.

Capital, Reconsidered

Traditionally, when we hear the word "capital" used, it is in relation to money. The most common definition of capital is "financial assets or the financial value of assets such as cash." But capital can also be defined more broadly:

- any form of wealth employed or capable of being employed in the production of more wealth
- any source of profit, advantage, power, etc.

Most businesses, when they talk about capital, are talking about the money they have available to invest in business opportunities. If a company had the opportunity to grow though the purchase of a competing company, it would prefer to use capital to make that purchase rather than incurring debt by borrowing the money to make the acquisition. Financial capital is a tool or a resource that can be used to accomplish business objectives.

The broader definition of capital refers to "wealth," which can be extended to any type of asset that could be used to create new value. An example commonly used in business today is "human capital." Human capital refers to the value of the collective knowledge, skills, experience, and abilities of the employees of an organization. A company with strong human capital could be assumed to have enough of the right kind of people to identify and exploit new opportunities. Human capital is an intangible asset and is therefore much more difficult to measure and quantify than the more tangible financial capital, but it is no less important. Without strong human capital, an organization might not be able to maximize the value of its financial capital, because the people who run the organization lack the ability or capacity to grow with the organization.

Recently, the concept of capital has been extended to another intangible asset: the value that exists in the relationships between people. This new form of capital is called "social capital."

Social Capital Defined

There are many definitions for social capital in use, and a quick Google search for the phrase pulls up several million hits.

- In *The Forms of Capital*, Pierre Bourdieu defines social capital as "the aggregate of the actual or potential resources which are linked to possession of a durable network of more or less institutionalised relationships of mutual acquaintance and recognition".[3]
- "Social capital refers to those stocks of social trust, norms, and networks that people can draw upon to solve common problems."[4]
- Robert Putnam, political scientist and author describes social capital as the "features of social organization, such as trust, norms, and networks, that can improve the efficiency of society by facilitating coordinated actions"[5]

All of these definitions and others help to build the conceptual framework for social capital, but each of them feels a bit technical and academic for our taste. Instead, we prefer the simple, straightforward definition presented by Wayne Baker in his book, *Achieving Success Through Social Capital*. He defines social capital as:

"The resources available in and through personal and business relationships."

These resources are a product of the number and nature of our relationships with others. They come in many forms and they can be used in many different ways (see sidebar for examples). It is important to understand that social capital, like other forms of capital, is something that can be grown, managed, and used in your efforts to make things happen personally and professionally. If we take a moment to reflect, it becomes quickly apparent how important social capital is in our lives.

Many of the things we do every day, often without thinking, somehow involve the use of our social capital, these resources available to us through our relationships with others.

Social capital can take many forms:

- **Information**: insight about new job opportunities, upcoming entertainment or community events that aren't common knowledge.

- **Opinion or reference**: how to find a good lawyer, doctor, or dentist or the best schools or restaurants.

- **Help and assistance**: someone to bail you out of jail or help you move.

- **Ideas and feedback**: referrals to business leads, creative suggestions and solutions.

- **Expertise**: help with taxes, computer troubleshooting.

- **Access to resources**: people who can donate to my charity, someone who runs a local gym for my daughter's volleyball practice.

Each of these forms can be extremely valuable, personally and professionally. This social capital can at times be more valuable than financial capital, because it can make things available to you that are not for sale. And all of this value exists within the network of connections and relationships you have with others.

Social capital sometimes works in less obvious ways. Consider this example. You get recruited to spend two evenings making some fundraising calls on behalf of a local charity that you support. On the first night, you are given a list of names and phone numbers for 20 people you do not know. On the second night, you are asked to call 20 people that you personally know and ask them for financial support. These two nights would probably be two very different experiences for you. It's likely that you would probably get some contributions on the first night from the people you don't know. But whether you raise $50 on your first evening or $500, none of it is due to social capital, because you do not know any of the people you are soliciting.

Assuming you are able to reach a similar number of people on the second night, we might expect that you would raise considerably more money because the people you call are people you know (and who know you). At the very least, it should be much easier to raise the same amount of money as the first night. In either case, the second night is an easier win because you have a certain amount of social capital with the people you call. The difference between knowing someone and not knowing someone can have a profound impact on the outcome of your interaction with them.

Sometimes we stumble upon connections and valuable social capital develops accidentally. Consider some of the key relationships for one of the most successful people on the planet, Bill Gates. Steve Ballmer, who is now CEO of Microsoft, first met Bill Gates at Harvard University where they lived just down the hall from each other. Melinda Gates, a former unit manager at Microsoft, met Bill Gates in 1987 at a company press event in Manhattan and eventually married him years later. Even Bill Gates and Warren Buffet met by coincidence and are now business and philanthropic partners, as well as friends.[6] What Gates and Buffet both seem to have figured out is how to take unexpected opportunities to connect with others and turn them into meaningful (and often profitable) relationships. Bill Gates and Warren Buffett have connection mindsets.

We regularly come into contact with new people, and we cannot possibly predict the potential that exists within each of these relationships. We happen upon social capital in the same way we occasionally come into unexpected financial capital by finding a $20 bill in a coat pocket or learning of an inheritance from a deceased family member or friend. While these events are largely beyond our control, we can influence and control a number of other, contributing factors if we are intentional about them. The person that closely manages his or her finances is likely to end up much better off financially than the person who might make more income but does not budget carefully. Discipline and clarity of purpose make all the difference. The same is true regarding social capital. If you appreciate the value of social capital and understand how it works, you can have a plan for becoming social capital rich.

By being disciplined and intentional about social capital, you can ensure that you have access to all the resources you need to achieve your goals. This book will provide you with guidance about how to do just that: *to successfully increase the resources available to you through your relationships with others*. You can do this regardless of your title, profession, gender, experience, level of education, or any other personal quality or status. Social capital is a level playing field. If you want to have more social capital tomorrow than you have today, you can make that happen. You do not need anyone's permission, and you do not need a budget or special training. You just need to make a choice. It's 100 percent up to you.

Harnessing Social Gravity

1. Write down at least three examples of times when you have used social capital to your advantage.

_____

_____

_____

2. Write down at least three examples of times when you needed social capital but didn't have any. Specifically note for each case what type of social capital you needed and what difference it would have made for you.

_____

_____

_____

3. Based on the examples and questions listed in this chapter, make two lists. In one list, name the areas where you feel you have strong social capital resources. In the second list, note the areas where you are social capital poor.

_____   _____

_____   _____

_____   _____

_____   _____

_____   _____

_____   _____

_____   _____

_____   _____

_____   _____

SOCIAL GRAVITY

CHAPTER 2

SURVEY SAYS: WHO YOU KNOW REALLY DOES MATTER, BUT WE DON'T LIKE IT

CONNECTED JASON

On May 17, 2010, I received a LinkedIn invitation to connect from someone I had never met. His name was Greg Harris and he was the president of a company based in Omaha called Quantum Workplace. Greg had included a note in his invitation that said, "I've heard your name come up several times in the last week. I'd like to add you to my network on LinkedIn." Since he provided me some context for his invitation, I happily accepted his connection and replied with a message of my own inviting him to have lunch. Greg's company sells a product for surveying employees, so his work was squarely in my area of interest.

A few weeks later, we got together for an early morning breakfast to get acquainted. We spent more than two hours talking, sharing ideas, and bouncing concepts back and forth. It was a great meeting and it was clear that Greg and I were meant to do some work together.

At one point in the conversation, he mentioned that his company was always looking for questions or concepts to test in its survey process. This comment led us down the path of doing the research you are about to read in this chapter. Social capital reveals itself in many different forms. This was a great one.

Thank you, LinkedIn.

"It's not what you know; it's who you know that matters." We open the book with this quote because it's the way that most people can best describe the pull of social gravity in their lives. From our experience, it seems that this phrase is pretty commonly thrown around. So, we wondered just how much people actually believed it and, more importantly, how they felt about it.

Since the majority of our professional lives have been spent working in the fields of human resources, leadership development, and diversity, we spend much of our time studying the dynamics of the workplace. Work is important. It's how we all earn our livings and pay for the stuff we want and need. Most of us spend more time working than doing any other single activity besides sleeping. So, this seemed like a natural place for us to research beliefs about social gravity.

In early 2010, we had the idea to gather some data for the book about how social gravity shows up in the workplace. In Greg Harris, President of Quantum Workplace, we found the perfect partner to help us gather this data and explore what kind of story it would tell us.

Quantum Workplace is in the employee data business. It is one of the leading organizations in the world at measuring employee engagement. In fact, its survey methodology powers the "Best Places to Work" programs in nearly 50 cities across the United States. It gathers employee opinion data from more than 4,000 companies annually, and its database represents literally millions of employee responses. Needless to say, we were thrilled to partner with such an industry powerhouse to collect our data.

So, in September 2010, we conducted our research. The survey consisted of a total of nine questions that were designed to gather employee opinions about the importance of networks and relationships in the workplace, particularly as it relates to getting ahead. We also designed some questions to probe how individuals feel about promotional decisions that are made based on relationships. Our survey sample includes 979 responses from employees at a wide range of employers in seven major U.S. cities. For those of you who are interested in seeing the actual survey questions, we've included those in Appendix 1 at the back of the book.

What We Heard

Our hypothesis was that most people recognize the importance of relationships but that they view it as unfair when others gain an advantage due to a relationship. Our experience told us that people are very conflicted over the power of relationships in their lives. The data seems to support this.

- **70 percent** of respondents agreed that it is important to have a strong network at work. Only 3 percent disagreed.

- **62 percent** agreed that an employee's skill at networking is valuable to both the employee and the organization. Yet, only 38 percent said that an employee's network of relationships at work should be considered in promotional decisions.

- **88 percent** agreed that knowing the right people is critical to getting promoted in their organizations, but a whopping 64 percent said it is unfair when someone gets promoted because of who they know at work.

The people in our survey seemed to recognize the importance of relationships and the value of networks. But, they had trouble taking the next step and embracing that the value of these networks should be directly rewarded through a promotion or in other ways.

When asked what factors are generally used to make promotional decisions within their organizations, the majority or respondents said that individual performance and leadership potential were most common, and most also agreed that these factors are appropriate. But, a significant 19.6 percent of respondents reported that the relationship between the employee and the decision maker was the most important factor being considered in their organizations for promotional decisions. When asked what criteria should be used to make promotional decisions at work, less than 3 percent chose the relationship between employee and decision maker. This seemed to reveal a belief that others are getting ahead because of relationships, and we don't like it. To understand why, we needed to dig a little further.

Who You Know Matters, But It's Not Fair

To ensure that we had plenty of insight to cull through, we asked one optional, open-ended question as a part of our survey. Here's the question we asked:

Please respond to the following cliché:

"Who you know is more important than what you know."
(e.g. do you agree? If so, is it fair?)

This question struck a nerve with many of the respondents. While the question was optional, 863 of the 979 people who took our survey decided to chime in with their thoughts. That's 88.2 percent or, more concretely, 33 pages of single-spaced text responses full of passion, opinion, and perceptions. We were thrilled that so many chose to share their opinions, because it provided a much more robust view of this topic.

Here is a sampling of the responses we received to the question above:

"It does appear that who you know will most likely get you into an organization rather than your experience or degree. This is just my observation over the years from close friends and my own personal journey to find a job. However, I don't agree with the cliché, because it makes going to college to better one's self irrelevant."

"You may be the best at what you do, but it does not matter if others do not realize your value or potential."

"This statement is a nice explanation of cronyism."

"I believe that who you know and what you know are equally important. That being said, if an organization is going to consider who their employees know as a major factor in promotions, the employer needs to provide opportunities for the employee to network, both inside and outside the organization."

"No it's not fair—but who said life should be fair? There are people who are much better at forging relationships than I am. They have a talent for working with people ... they should get ahead."

"I totally disagree with this. Individual knowledge and performance should be a deciding factor in achievement."

"Who you know allows you to get your foot in the door, but your skills and performance have to speak for themselves afterwards."

"Often people who are climbing the ladder via who they know are threatened by others who have more knowledge and a better understanding of the big picture. That's when we end up with bosses who have no idea what their staff members know, have no interest in learning, and run around scared to death while trying to please their bosses by setting higher and higher goals for an already maxed-out staff. We end up with a narcissistic hierarchy of bosses who have no idea what is truly humanly possible and who every day in every way let their staff know that nothing they do is good enough."

"I agree with this as, at every job I have ever had, the people who do the work are not recognized or promoted; only the people who know and 'suck up' to the higher-ups get promoted. This attitude is patently wrong, as upper management is populated by toadies who do not have the skills, knowledge, or experience to lead the company and/or department into meeting the goals of the organization."

"I am so sick of seeing people promoted because they kiss ass. It would be nice to see someone get a promotion because they work hard."

"It is not fair, but it is the way it is."

"I think my relationships with people inside each organization helped me advance greatly. I think it's fair in the sense that people who know a lot of people are putting in the time to network. It's only unfair if it's a nepotism situation or based purely on friendship and not performance."

"I have worked for 43 years and have seen people promoted and hired based on their personal relationships. Predominantly these people are ineffective, lack any work ethic, [are] emotionally challenged, etc. Ergo this is not fair and proves detrimental to the organization."

"Hockey Puck!!! So you know the big man at the top. Does that make you qualified to handle a difficult task? I don't think so.

"Not all people have the capability or the need to social network. Some people work very hard and have great work ethics but are not noticed because they do not chat and 'network.'"

"It is a lot easier to 'wow' the right people if you know who to impress. No, it's not fair, but it's how the world works."

"I think that who you know is important. Someone looking for a leadership position should be meeting people within the organization, especially those in higher level positions. I think that individual performance is also relevant and that someone must be doing their job well to grow in the organization. At the same time, cultivating a network within the organization is also key to learning about areas for growth and pursuing higher opportunities."

"I certainly believe that developing good relationships with individuals outside of one's immediate work area will better position an employee to take advantage of potential opportunity for promotion. Networking is important; however, 'who you know' should not influence an employer in who they choose to fill a specific position."

"Knowing the right people always increases your chances for success and, if partnered with 'what you know,' your success increases."

"I don't think it is necessarily unfair. It is up to the individual to network and promote themselves to create good opportunities. If you don't take the time to build a strong network, you will likely miss out on many opportunities."

"In this day and age, the cliché still rings true. I am in my present position because of a referral from a friend. Though my qualifications well meet the duties of the position, my 'foot in the door' came from 'who I know.'"

"Unfortunately, this is true. I've seen too many promotions based on sucking up instead of the work the person did."

"It is sad but true. In our society, no one seems to care about sacrifice with regards to securing the necessary skills, certification, and/or education to get ahead. It's all about 'you scratch my back and I will scratch yours!' It is not fair, but what are you to do?"

"I strongly disagree. It should be about what you know instead of who you know. It is not fair and it isn't right."

"Who you know at work is important in advancement with a company, because it shows your strengths not only within yourself but [also] your determination in putting your name 'out there' and being recognized for your accomplishments. I believe it also exudes confidence."

"I used to think I could get by on my own merit, but it really is about who you know."

"I would like to think it is not true, but I am being naive. It is not fair."

"Totally disagree. However, the ability to create strong working relationships with all that you interact with is very important."

"I agree with the above statement, but it is not fair. I do think it is very important to be able to get along well with others and try to build a relationship with coworkers. It shows leadership ability and builds a strong foundation for the company."

"I do not believe that it is only about having connections in 'high' places. ... You have to have a network of people who are aware of your skills and qualifications, and who are able to speak on your behalf to the quality of your work, leadership style, ethics, etc."

"Today's young professionals are more educated than ever before. Their greatest accomplishment is developing a network enabling them to quickly and seamlessly achieve that next big step in their future. Who you know far surpasses what you know. ... Anyone can learn new skills to perform, but it doesn't really matter if you don't have a chance to make that move."

"You may not have the full credentials that they are looking for (e.g., bachelor's degree), but if you have the experience and you are well known throughout the organization for doing a good job, I think you would be a good qualifier."

"It's all about being a manipulator and suck-up when it comes to climbing up the ladder."

Overall, these responses further supported our hypothesis that people do recognize the importance of relationships and further revealed that they don't like it when relationships are considered in promotional decisions. But since these were open-ended responses, we were able to discover some more hints as to why this conflict exists.

In summary, here is what the responses showed:

- Most people realize that who you know is important and that it impacts decisions in the workplace, but they don't seem to be actively using that knowledge to their advantage.

- "It's not what you know, but who you know that matters" has a highly negative connotation in many people's minds. A majority equated it with "sucking up, " "kissing ass, " nepotism, and favoritism.

- It is assumed by many that those who get ahead through who they know are incompetent.

- People in general seem to be naïve to the impact that relationships have on the way work gets done. They clearly don't see "networking" or relationships as part of their jobs or as having anything to do with their job performance.

- People strongly believe that it is not fair when who you know matters in decisions regarding getting ahead in work and life.

- Those who seem to embrace "it's who you know" as a way of life or as the way things work have less-frequent perceptions of unfair treatment.

- Many people recognize the importance of who you know when it comes to getting a job interview, a foot in the door, or for being considered for a promotion. What they don't seem to recognize is the effect it has on their day-to-day lives and how they get work done.

Our Conclusion

Taken in whole, the survey data supported what we thought was the case: people can feel the effects of social gravity at work, but they don't know how to take advantage of it to benefit themselves. People know that relationships matter and that they are important. No surprises there. What might be surprising is that, despite this belief, there is strong resentment when relationships seem to result in an advantage or reward. A majority of people feel that it is unfair when relationships enter into decisions about advancement at work. Why the disconnect?

It might be helpful to step back for a moment and consider the notion of "fairness." The word fair by definition usually means either free from injustice (e.g., a fair decision) or proper under the rules (e.g., a fair fight). So, technically, if something is "unfair" it represents an injustice or, worse, cheating. But, there's another common way that fairness is often used that doesn't show up in the formal definition. Many times, when people (and particularly children) say something isn't fair, they are reacting not about a violation of the rules but rather to the perceived injustice that they didn't know the rules (e.g., "I didn't know that you were going to give a surprise cash bonus for staying late to do extra work today when I snuck out early. That's just not fair."). In this context, there is a perception of injustice, but it's based on a personal sense of loss stemming from either a lack of knowledge or just plain ignorance.

It is in this way that we feel people are using the word "fair" as they describe their reaction to the "it's not what you know" cliché. Most people are never taught the skills of networking. They don't know how to harness this force of social gravity to use it to their advantage. So, when they see someone else who does, they feel as though they losing in a game they don't really know how to play. This might be how you feel and why you picked up this book. Our observation based on both this research and our own experience is that the higher degree of skill one possesses at networking and building relationships—thus harnessing social gravity—the less likely that person is to feel that it's unfair when others get an advantage because of it. Instead of thinking "that's not fair," they instead think "I need to find a way to build those kinds of relationships."

If you think there are times when the inappropriate consideration of relationships in promotional decisions is unfair, you are right. Certainly, favoritism and nepotism are alive and well within the workplace. And promotional decisions made on this basis are likely unfair. So, some of the disconnect that appears in this data may also be partially fueled by perceptions related to how relationships factor into promotion decisions. It seems to be commonly accepted that a strong network can make a person more effective and more influential, but it appears that most people don't trust managers or leaders to make the appropriate distinction.

To further explore this point, we sorted the results of the survey by employee-engagement level. For those unfamiliar with the concept of employee engagement level, here is how Quantum Workplace defines and measures it:

> **Employee Engagement is the tendency of employees to exert discretionary effort for the benefit of the organization, their intent to stay, and their tendency to speak highly of the organization. Engaged employees feel valued, enjoy their roles, and see how their work contributes to the success of the organization. They see harmony between their goals and those of the organization and they trust their managers and the senior leaders of the organization.**

Engagement simply measures how eager an employee is to come to work and help the company succeed by giving extra effort beyond what's required for the job. When we took a look at our data through the lens of employee engagement, here's what we found:

Highly engaged employees seem to have a better sense of the importance of relationships to work, and they are more comfortable with relationships being a part of promotional decisions than are their disengaged peers.

Highly engaged employees also seem less worried about the impact of relationships on their own ability to get promoted. They were less concerned about the "fairness" of considering relationships when it came time for promotions.

The correlation on these issues was pretty clear. Highly engaged employees are more tuned into the role that relationships play at work, and they embrace it more than employees who are less engaged.

In the end, this research points to two major conclusions:

- People know relationships are important, but they aren't sure what to do about it.

- People feel that getting ahead through "who you know" is unfair because they don't know how to get the relationships they need to create their own advantage.

This is why we wrote this book. Social gravity is how we describe the role relationships play in our lives. It affects everyone, and everyone has the opportunity to harness it for their own good. By studying the forces of social gravity and learning more about how and why relationships form and grow, any person can find success in his or her work and life. That's the irony. It's both what you know *and* who you know that matters.

It's now time for you to gain the knowledge you need to unleash the power of social gravity in your life.

SOCIAL GRAVITY

CHAPTER 3:

ANATOMY OF A NETWORK

Do you know where your relationships come from?

Social capital is "the resources available through personal and business relationships." This seems simple enough on the surface, but just as human beings are complex and dynamic, the relationships between human beings can be complex and dynamic. If we are to fully harness the power of social capital in our lives, we can likely benefit from a deeper understanding of the types and nature of these relationships.

We frequently use the term "connection" to represent a type of relationship between two people. For our purposes, connection is a first step in the process of building a more substantial relationship like an acquaintance or friend. A connection is where the seeds of a potential relationship are planted. By our definition, a connection is established once two people meet (whether online or in person), exchange at least some level of information with one another, and leave the interaction equipped with a means to easily get back in touch with each other. So, by this definition, if two people interact through Twitter in the process of exchanging thoughts about an upcoming baseball game and then send each other their email addresses for future correspondence, they have formed a connection. On the other hand, if you introduce two of your acquaintances at a cocktail party and they ultimately part ways without exchanging any further information, a connection is not made between these two people. Certainly, there was an opportunity for connection there, but no connection was made. A connection requires more than mere knowledge of each other; instead, there must be some scaffolding in place for further interaction, such as the exchange of contact information or plans to interact further.

Connections are a beginning. It's important to make connections, but what happens after a connection is critical in the formation of social capital. Many types of relationships can blossom from a connection. Let's begin with one that we can all relate to: friendship.

The Friendship Factor

When most of us think about our connections, we generally think first of our friends. After all, our friends are the people we know the best and see most often. From a social capital perspective, it's pretty easy to put value on the types of relationships we have with our friends. They provide us with camaraderie, support, and encouragement. Our friends were there when we met our soul mate and they were there for us when we got fired. Friends are an important component of our social networks, and they play a variety of important roles in our lives.

Because our friends are such an important part of our network, it's worth taking a look at where these friendships come from. In our presentations on this topic, we ask our audiences this question:

What do you think is the most significant factor in determining who we become friends with?

If you are like most people, you probably think that you have selected your friends because they share your interests and values. Since our best friends play such an important role in our lives, we like to think that we must have intentionally and thoughtfully selected who fills this important role for us. The real answer is quite different.

Take a moment to create a list of your three or four closest friends in the chart below. Once you have the names written down, recall for each one of them how you originally met, and write that down in the second column. Did you grow up together as neighbors? Did you sit next to each other in school or college? Maybe you met each other at work?

MY CLOSEST FRIENDS	HOW WE MET

Contrary to what we might expect, the most significant factor in determining who we become friends with is physical proximity. We literally become closest to those who are physically closest to us. There is extensive research that suggests that this is the case starting as early as elementary school. One research study from 1955 found that children were more likely to become friends with those who they sat next to in class than with their classmates in general.[7] This effect holds true even into the college years according, to a 2008 study of college freshmen.[8] This study was designed to examine whether "randomly determined physical proximity and group assignment during an initial encounter" would have a significant effect on the formation of friendships. The researchers summarized their findings this way:

> **"In a nutshell, people may become friends simply because they drew the right random number. Thus, becoming friends may indeed be due to chance."**

Beyond the classroom, it appears that who we live next to has an effect on who we choose as friends as well. In one of the more famous studies on this topic, the friendships of individuals living in student housing at Massachusetts Institute of Technology were examined to determine the extent to which proximity affected friendships. The study found that 65 percent of the friends studied lived in the same building. Of these, 44 percent of the friends lived next door to one another and another 22 percent lived two doors apart.[9] Proximity clearly has a powerful affect on who we choose as our friends. Consider the role of proximity in the connection between Bill Gates and Steve Ballmer mentioned earlier.

Now, let's revisit our own experiment involving our friends. Look at your list of close friends above. Did you find like we did that most of your friendships were formed with people who you spent time being physically close to? Most people typically discover that their friendships originally started with people they sat next to in class or at work or perhaps with a childhood neighbor or even a cousin who you saw frequently at family gatherings. Why is this important? As we begin to think about the power and value of our social capital, we must examine the type of information and connections those closest to us possess and how that compares to our own.

Friendships are important. It is our friends that help us move our furniture, pick our partners, and advise us on careers and life choices. Friends bail us out of jail and tell us things others would not. But, since it seems that our friends generally occupy the same relatively small physical spaces that we do, they may not be a great source of new information, ideas, or connections. As we saw above, our friends likely work with us, live next door to us, or work out at the same gyms as we do. It's for this reason that the brilliant author Malcolm Gladwell argues in his book *The Tipping Point* that our acquaintances, those people who we know but who are not close friends with, are a unique source of social influence and power.

The Strength of Weak Ties

To drive home his assertion about the power of acquaintances, Gladwell refers to a seminal study done in 1974 by Mark Granovetter titled "Getting a Job." It was in this study that Granovetter put forth his famous theory called "the strength of weak ties. " Granovetter studied several hundred professional workers in a Boston suburb regarding their employment history. Of the individuals he interviewed, he found that 56 percent of them found their jobs through a personal connection of some sort, 19 percent found their jobs through a more formal means such as advertising or headhunters, and roughly 20 percent had applied directly to the company to get their job. None of this probably is terribly surprising. In fact, a Forrester Research study found that of those job searchers today who use the internet in their job search, 96 percent of them end up finding their jobs in other ways besides the internet. Of that 96 percent, about 40 percent found their jobs through a personal referral or similar source.[10] If you've had the experience of looking for a job, as most of us have, it's not uncommon to hear that "the best jobs aren't advertised." The perception (if not the reality) is that the most sought-after jobs are generally filled through word of mouth. Both the Granovetter and Forrester research suggest that this is true.

But Granovetter's study found something much more interesting when he examined the types of connections involved with helping the 56 percent of his study participants find their jobs. Intriguingly, only 16.7 percent of this referring group reported that the people who provided the contacts to help them get their jobs were people who they saw as often as one would see a close friend. His research found that, in a majority of cases, the individuals who played the key role in helping the job seekers get their jobs were people who they saw either occasionally (55.6 percent) or even rarely (28 percent). Think about that for a moment. A person that you see rarely is *twice* as likely to connect you with a great job than your close friend. This study proved that, at least for job searching, the people with whom we share weak ties are the most meaningful source of important information. Since these "weak ties," or acquaintances, typically have access to different information and knowledge than our "close ties" or friends, they are the best source of new information, ideas, and contacts.

Let's again think about our own friends for a moment. Friends are important to us, but their importance is not likely to come in the form of new or different information or ideas. If you are like most people, many of your friends probably also know each other and may even socialize together with or without you. As you think about these friends, it's also likely that they may live, work, worship, or play much like you do. Think now of someone you have talked to recently who you do not know very well. Did that person seem to know about things that you didn't? If not, you may not have asked the right questions to unlock the information that person had to share.

Quantity and Quality – The Overlap

With the evolution of social networking sites like Facebook and LinkedIn, it's easier than ever before to make connections. It's not uncommon for an individual to have hundreds of "friends" on Facebook. But, are these friends really our friends?

The simple illustration below is helpful in understanding the difference between a simple connection and a more robust relationship between two people.

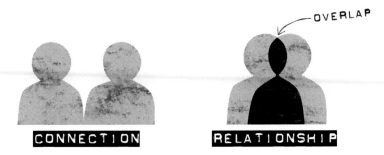

The actual relationship is the overlap between the two icons representing the two people. That is where the substance is, and that is what has been shared. Making the initial connection just brings those two people together. Very little has been shared, but an avenue has been created for sharing in the future. Through the connection exists an opportunity for relationship building.

It is space where the people overlap where the relationship lives. This overlap is where context and shared experience is stored. It is the pathway through which information and resources ebb and flow from one person to another. In this overlap, you may also find trust, history, and expectations between the two individuals. While this is easy to see in the diagram, in actual relationships, this overlap is generally unspoken and simply the product of individual behaviors between two people.

To build social capital, it's important to focus not only on the number of connections we make but also on the actions we take to create overlap with those connections and convert them into relationships. If you are not trying to increase that overlap with your connections, then you are placing a disproportionate emphasis on quantity in your network. We will look further at this in Chapter 10.

This book's authors have shared a variety of experiences over the past decade or more. These experiences have been both personal and professional. Our two circles overlap a lot. We are business partners and friends. Jason was the best man in Joe's wedding. Because of our history, we easily and fluidly navigate our collaborative work and make decisions about what to do next. This is the power of the overlap.

It is important and valuable to add new people to your network. But it is also important to continue to invest in the relationships you have with the people that you are already connected to.

The human brain consists of billions of neurons, each with several thousand synaptic connections to other neurons. When you perform a task, think about something, or have an experience, your brain accesses specific networks of connected neurons. The more often you use a particular combination of neurons, the easier it is for you to access that particular combination again, when needed. In memorizing a poem or learning a magic trick, you activate a particular combination of neurons numerous times as you practice. After doing this work, you can quickly and easily access that memory or ability at will. Without the repetition or practice, however, your access starts to fade, as the neural connections involved start to weaken. Go long enough without exercising a connection and it may fade away almost completely.

The connections that you have with other people are in many ways similar to the connections in your brain. You and each of the other people you are connected to are like neurons. The neurons in your brain are linked to other neurons by synapses, and you are linked to other people in your network through interactions. Some of those connections between you and other people are strong and others are weak. The healthier the pathway is between you and another person, the easier for you both to remember it is there and the easier it is for both of you to use it.

Imagine for a second that a couple of weeks ago you went to an open house for a new business being launched by a friend of yours. At that open house you were introduced to two people that were already sitting at a table together, Sandy and Max. The three of you spend some time getting to know each other and have a nice conversation about a variety of things, and at the end of the evening you all exchange contact information.

The following day you get an email invitation from Sandy to join her LinkedIn network. You open up the invitation, view Sandy's LinkedIn profile for a minute, and accept the invitation to join her LinkedIn network. This brings Sandy and your conversation the previous evening back to mind (kind of like lighting up a network of neurons again). The following day you receive an email message from Sandy with a link to a blog and a short message saying that she wanted to recommend one of her favorite blogs to you because, based on your initial conversation, it seemed like something that you might also enjoy. This again brings Sandy to mind and creates more overlap between the two of you: more shared context, more actual relationship. A couple of days later when you find out about an opportunity that might be of value to someone else, Sandy will likely come to mind because of the simple exchanges you have shared since first meeting. The pathway between the two of you has been "lit up" multiple times. But, since you've never had any follow up with Max, who you met at the same time as Sandy, he could easily fade from your memory.

Quality Versus Quantity

In building a vibrant and valuable network of relationships, it is important not to lose sight of the difference between quantity of connections and quality of connections. As we learned from Gladwell and Granovetter, acquaintances who we don't know all that well can be a tremendous source of social capital. Thus, we might assume that the best strategy is to make as many acquaintances as possible. But, we also know that we have to create overlap in relationships in order to unlock the true value. So, the right approach is to pursue both: increasing quantity of connections while at the same time increasing the overlap in those relationships by building quality and depth.

Now for the bad news. You will never be able to meet everyone, even if you make it your full-time job. Further, you also cannot invest in a deep and profound relationship with everyone that you meet. Not only are you limited in how much time and energy you can apply to building relationships, but you also face some limits regarding how many connections you can wrap your brain around. In fact, there's actually some science to the number of relationships humans can maintain, and it's called Dunbar's number.

Dunbar's number is a theoretical cognitive limit to the number of people with whom one can maintain stable social relationships. These are relationships in which an individual knows who each person is and how each person relates to every other person. Proponents assert that numbers larger than this generally require more restrictive rules, laws, and enforced norms to maintain a stable, cohesive group. No precise value has been proposed for Dunbar's number. It lies between 100 and 230, but a commonly detected value is 150.

Dunbar's number was first proposed by British anthropologist Robin Dunbar, who theorized that "this limit is a direct function of relative neocortex size, and that this in turn limits group size ... the limit imposed by neocortical processing capacity is simply on the number of individuals with whom a stable inter-personal relationship can be maintained." On the periphery, the number also includes past colleagues such as high school friends with whom a person would want to reacquaint themselves if they met again.[11]

This theory does not suggest that we can only know 150 people, because most of us do know far more people than that. Instead, it suggests that there is a mental limit to the number of active social relationships we can maintain and that, when we push beyond that maximum, our ability to maintain those social relationships starts to diminish. In addition to these cognitive limits, we also have a limited amount of time and energy. The acts of reaching out to people, meeting people, keeping track of people, and learning more about those people all take time and energy. There are only so many hours in the day, and we have to balance relationship building with all of the other responsibilities of our lives.

You have probable felt the impact of Dunbar's number in your life. A common example can be the difference between working for a small company where you know everyone in the company versus working for a large employer where you may only know those in your office or department. One company, W. L. Gore Associates, many years ago took an innovative approach to combatting this effect as the company grew. Gore is a manufacturing company headquarterd in Newark, Delaware. The companie's founder, Bill Gore, and his organization have been widely recognized for their innovative management practices.

This company operates under what it calls a "lattice" organizational model, in which employees choose what projects they want to work on and there aren't any formal organizational charts or titles. To make this kind of organization work requires healthy and trusting relationships between all employees. Gore discovered very early on that when a plant grew to between 150 and 200 people, the effectiveness of the system began to break down because the people didn't know each other well. So, the company made it policy for many years to build a new facility when one reached that critical number of people. This ensured that all of the people working together within each plant could know each other and be invested in one another socially. Gore had found a way to embrace Dunbar's number, even in a larger, growing organization. And it seems to have worked. Today, W.L. Gore is 53 years old, with $2.6 billion in yearly revenue and 9,000 employees, and has been named to the *Fortune* magazine's "100 Best Companies to Work For" list for 12 consecutive years.

Dunbar's number is very powerful beyond the walls of organizations. It limits who we can keep close in our own personal networks as well. So, the reality is that each of us has limits regarding what and how much we can do to build our social capital. Those limits are different for each of us depending on our stage of life or our profession, but we all have them and they are important to understand, because they play a major role in how we individually build social capital.

We have no magic solution to offer to remove or lessen those limitations. Through the application of time management and technology, you may be able to expand your limits a little, but you will always have limited resources to invest in creating and managing social capital. Time management can be a powerful tool, but it is not about putting more time in your life. Rather, it is about being more efficient, intentional, and strategic about working within your constraints. Our intent is to help you more effectively work with the time and resources that you have. Doing so boils down to making important choices about where (and with whom) you focus your energy and attention. To provide a framework for making those choices, we are going to examine three characteristics that can help you better identify people that might be of special value to your network.

Harnessing Social Gravity

1. Make a list of the most important 20 relationships in your life. Then, note for each relationship the amount of overlap that exists in that relationship today.

_____   _____

_____   _____

_____   _____

_____   _____

_____   _____

_____   _____

_____   _____

_____   _____

_____   _____

_____   _____

2. Evaluate the list above to determine the three relationships in which increasing overlap would have the greatest impact on your social capital. Write down three ideas for how you might increase overlap with each.

_____

_____

_____

_____

3. Think about where you spend time and where you do not spend time. How might where you spend time be impacting whom you become friends with? Can you find examples on how the proximity of where you spend your time has impacted the makeup of your network and friends?

_____

_____

_____

_____

_____

_____

_____

_____

_____

CHAPTER 4:

WHERE THE POWER LIES

CONNECTED JASON

Many years ago, I was in the process of moving from one apartment to another. Since I live some distance from my family and had only lived in town for about a year, I had to rely on my new friends in the area for help moving my furniture. As I prepared for the move, I reached out to a list of six or eight people who I thought might be willing to help me out. I thought for certain I'd have a small army to help.

When the morning of the move arrived, I backed up the truck to the door of my building and started hauling out small boxes. I assumed that my help would start arriving at any moment. As I made more and more trips to the truck by myself, I started to get a sinking feeling in my stomach. No one was coming to help me move. This was a problem, because I had several things that I couldn't move by myself.

Finally, my phone rang at about 10 a.m. It was my friend and former boss Randy. He had been out of town with his family and had gotten tangled up in a snowstorm. He was calling to see if I was still going to need some help when he got back to town in the early afternoon. I thanked him profusely for calling and asked that he come over when he could to help me move the big stuff from one place to the other.

As I reflected on this experience and got over the initial disappointment of how unreliable my new "friends" seemed to be, it became pretty clear to me that having a big network didn't do me much good if I didn't have anybody in that network who would help me move furniture.

A good friend will always bail you out of jail when you call them. A true friend will be sitting right next you in jail saying "Damn, that was fun."

-Unknown

Malcolm Gladwell wrote one of the most popular books on social networks in recent years, The Tipping Point. The book is built around the consideration of how ideas spread and why some ideas catch on and others don't. The underlying argument in the book is that the spread of ideas happens in the same way as viruses, from person to person. When viruses spread in a certain way, they reach a "tipping point" at which the rate of spread increases exponentially, resulting in an epidemic. Gladwell demonstrates how the spread of ideas works in this same way. One of the patterns that Gladwell relies on in his analysis is the Pareto principle, or the 80-20 rule. Also known as the law of the vital few, the Pareto principle generally means most things in life are not distributed evenly. The numbers 80 and 20 refer to outputs and inputs; simply stated, 20 percent of the people involved do 80 percent of the work. More generally, in any system, there are a small number of things that make a big difference. Consider a basketball team of 10 players. Based on the rules, only five players can play at one time. And, on any given basketball team, there will be two or three players who score the majority of the points and make a majority of the most important plays. The other players are important to the team, but remove those two or three key players and the results of the team will change dramatically. You have probably experienced the Pareto principle firsthand as a member of a committee or planning team in which much of the work was done by a few key members.

Gladwell explains how the Pareto principle is in effect in the spread of a virus, idea, or cause. In each case, there is generally a small group of people that play a very important role in reaching the tipping point. For the spread of ideas, he specifically identifies three of these unique roles for people whom he labels connectors, mavens, and salespeople. Gladwell outlines the role of each and the significance each plays in reaching the tipping point. The significance underlying his message is that, if you are in the idea or change business, rather than applying your efforts to spread your idea evenly over all people, you would be better served to invest your energy in finding and enlisting the help of connectors, mavens, and salespeople. Investing time with these people would be a more strategic investment of time because of their abilities to profoundly influence others.

It is this idea that translates to the creation of social capital. If our goal is to become social capital rich, we must invest our limited time and energy in making the right kinds of connections first. Then, we must develop overlap with the right people among those connections. Remember the Pareto principle: there are a small number of people in your network who deliver large amounts of resources and value to you. You can make enormous increases to your social capital by bringing more of those kinds of people into your network. It is important to meet new people, and we often do not know much about people initially, but as we go about building overlap we have to prioritize our efforts. If I met 10 new people last week, I might be better served by investing an additional hour in connecting with one of them than by investing an additional 10 minutes in each of them. Thus, it becomes necessary to have a framework for making those decisions.

All Connections are Not Created Equal

To identify those people who might add the most value to your network, you may have to think about people and connections a bit more analytically than you are used to. While most people are used to silently assessing others regularly on their perceived intelligence and attractiveness, it is a wholly different exercise to assess an individual's perceived value or potential value to your network. But, given that social capital is the key to success and resources are limited for both maintaining relationships and investing in them, those who are most successful at building social capital are those who are intentional about who they bring into their networks of connections.

Salespeople, due to the nature of their jobs, are probably the most focused about the value of who they bring into their networks. Earlier in Jason's career, he worked for an organization that was undergoing a significant software upgrade project. The project required that Jason's human resources team find and hire a large number of software programmers. News of the project spread quickly throughout the community, and soon every salesperson at organizations that provided technology-staffing services wanted to be his friend. He was constantly flooded with invitations to play golf, attend baseball games, or have lunch. Two years later, when the project was completed, these friendships faded and the invitations stopped. This wasn't because these salespeople didn't like Jason, but rather it was because they didn't perceive him to represent the value to their networks that he once did.

While the word value is used a lot, its true meaning seems to have gotten lost. When we talk about value, we are talking about the relative worth of a specific connection versus another. This may sound callous, but not all connections are created equal. Relative worth means that, when you compare 10 people who are potential connections, if you assume that it takes the same amount of effort to connect to each of them, some of those connections can bring more resources to your social capital than others. These connections represent greater potential value to your network. For the mathematically inclined, here's the equation:

| Amount of resources individual can add to my social capital | − | Amount of resources invested to make the connection | = | Social Capital Value |

Certainly, there are a lot of reasons that someone can add value to your network. We outlined a bunch of them in Chapter 1. Here, in consideration of the Pareto principle, we are taking about how to find individuals who add disproportionately large value to our networks compared to the average connection. As you consider the value an individual brings to your social capital, you should consider what they bring in three categories:

- Reach
- Power
- Diversity

We will describe each of the factors and give you tools to help recognize these as you begin the process of being more intentional about adding people to your network.

Reach

The first factor to consider as you look for individuals who could make major deposits into your social capital is reach. An example of a person with great reach is our friend Roger Fransecky. Roger is a man who has had a remarkable career that includes having been a clinical psychologist, university professor, CEO, and consultant. Roger's career has taken him to all corners of the world, where he has worked with people of all types and statures. As a result of his curiosity about people and a magnetic charm, Roger has created quite the personal network throughout his career. The striking thing about Roger as you get to know him is that he seems to have boundless resources and connections literally all around the world. He is as likely to introduce you to the owner of the wine shop down the street as he is to connect you to the CEO of a Fortune 500 company. Roger's network has tremendous reach.

Simply described, reach is the extent to which an individual is connected to others and thus represents potential introductions and future connections. To understand the impact of reach on your network, we're going to get analytical, but we believe that the value of Reach is intuitively understood. If you have met someone who connected you to a lot of other people you did not already know, you have benefited from someone's reach. We have both developed relationships with people that have generated a constant stream of new connections over several years. We have found people with large networks that have been willing to cross-pollinate their networks with ours. Whereas Dunbar's number suggests that we can only have an active network of 150 relationships at a time, the concept of Reach can help us understand how one group of 150 people might not represent the same value in terms of social capital as another group. If your network is composed of primarily people who work with you in the same office building, the reach of your network will be very different than if your network is full of people like Roger Fransecky. Reach adds power to a network.

Over the past decade, we have witnessed the increasing popularity of tools for social-network mapping and social-network analysis. Social-network maps are being used in the study of social capital, how information travels, how innovation happens, how behavior changes, how viruses spread, and other related topics. Essentially, social-network mapping consists of making a visual map of the relationships that exist within an organization or group of people. A social-network map can be built and drawn using sophisticated and specialized tools, or it can be drawn on the back of a napkin. It can serve as a visual representation of who knows who within a network or community. It can also provide information about the types of relationships involved and roles played by different members of the network. Regardless of how they are created, these maps give you a valuable picture of how people are connected.

Why a Map?

If you have lived in the same community for several years, you most likely know your way around and can even provide directions to other folks that are not as familiar with the area. Despite your familiarity with how your community is laid out, you can still benefit from looking at a map. When you look at a map, you may see routes or places you'd forgotten about. You may even be reminded of places you've been in the past and that you had forgotten. A map provides you with a different perspective of what is all around you. A social-network map works in a similar fashion by allowing you to step back and take a look at a visual rendering of relational information about the networks that exist all around you. Anything that makes the invisible visible or provides you with a different perspective can be valuable toward better decision making.

At its most basic, a social-network map is just a set of dots (each representing a person) and connecting lines (which represent connections between people). Social-network maps, when analyzed, can be a rich source of information about the functioning of a group of people, telling us things that do not show up on a traditional organizational chart or chain of command. Let's look at the example on the right.

Without any sophisticated tools or training, we can look at this social-network map and it becomes immediately clear that there are people playing very different roles within the network. In the above diagram we can see, for instance, that Susan plays a unique role in the middle of a cluster that contains most of the network. She has six direct connections, far more than anyone else in this

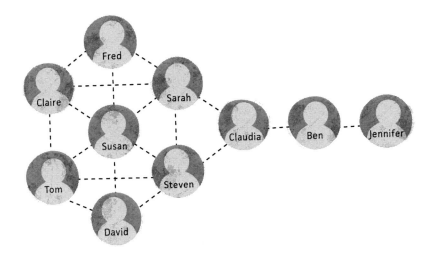

network cluster. Another person playing a unique role would be Claudia because she connects people in the network that would otherwise not be connected.

Social-network maps make the invisible visible and reveal additional information about the people in a network of relationships. This can be of value to us in thinking about how to identify and engage with them. We don't suggest that you need to become an expert in social-network mapping. Nor do we suggest that you need to start mapping out your network (although it's not a bad idea). Rather, we hope that the idea of social-network mapping will help you think differently about the people in your network or, equally important, the people you want to add to your your network. If you consider the example above, which person in the map might be the most valuable to add to your network?

We would suggest that based on this map you would probably want to add Susan. Claudia does provide a bridge, but Susan is a connector for several other people. By connecting to her, we are now one introduction away from the six others in the map who she's connected to.

To use a specific term, Susan has greater reach than others in her network because she's connected to more people. Reach represents the capability an individual has to connect others together. The larger (and more diverse) a person's network, the more potentially valuable they are to your network. People with great reach represent great potential social capital because of the access to people and other networks that they represent. Due to this fact, it's valuable to add people with large reach to your network.

Exponential Power of Networks

One of the most important characteristics of a network of relationships is that it is exponential in nature. This is part of what makes your network very powerful. The number of people that you are directly and indirectly connected to through your network gets big in a hurry. When you connect to a new person, you are not just connecting to that person alone but also creating a bridge into that person's network of relationships. This characteristic of networks is what gives life to the concept of "six degrees of separation" theory, the idea that a single person is no more than six connections removed from any other person on the planet.

Let's assume for the moment that you have 50 direct connections in your network. These are people that you have met, would recognize by sight, and readily know how to reach. Some of these are close ties and some are weak ties. Let's assume that each of those people also has 50 connections besides you. That would mean that through your 50 direct connections, you are connected to 2,550 people at only two degrees of separation. Going out a little bit further to three degrees of separation, if each of those second-degree connections has 50 connections, you would now have access to 127,550 people through your 50 direct connections. You would only need two introductions to reach any one of those 120,000-plus people. You probably already have more than 50 direct connections. Having 50 direct connections is a conservative number, but this simple example shows you how big the numbers can get quickly.

Now consider if you add people to your network who have extensive reach. These might be people who work in sales or politics and who as a requirement of their jobs must know and maintain at least basic relationships with hundreds of people. They could also be people who are highly skilled at online networking or who have blogs that are widely read by thousands of people. Adding one new contact with extensive reach to your network can actually provide you with indirect access to millions of new people. Think about it. If you replace the number 50 in the example above with 100, the number of potential connections increases from 127,550 to more than 1 million. That's a lot of potential value to add to your personal social capital.

CONNECTED JOE

So it really is a small world after all. The popular online social networking site LinkedIn gives us a good real-life example of how the numbers play out. For those who are unfamiliar with LinkedIn, like most social networks, it allows you to sign up for free and build a profile. Then you begin to build your network of connections by inviting people to connect to you on the site. In addition, once your profile is created, you will likely get requests from others to connect to them. These people become your direct connections on LinkedIn. As of late 2011, Joe had 1,136 connections on LinkedIn. And if Joe was looking for some information, insight on how to get a consulting gig with Google or recommendations on where to stay when he and his wife

travel to Bar Harbor, Maine, or how to go about selecting a virtual assistant, this would be a pretty good network of people to ask for advice. It is a fairly large group of people and they come from a variety of professions, industries, and geographies. LinkedIn also makes it very easy to reach out to your direct connections and others on LinkedIn. It is likely that someone in this network can be helpful to Joe.

Where things get really interesting is when we consider Joe's network beyond those direct connections. LinkedIn is designed to both facilitate direct connections like those described above and also allow users to share one another's networks. Specifically, LinkedIn allows you to see those people who your direct connections are connected to (second-degree connections) and who those people are connected to (third-degree connections). The site allows you to search and view all of these connections for the purpose of facilitating further connections and introductions. It is this functionality on LinkedIn that reveals the exponential power of networks.

Let's return to considering Joe's LinkedIn network. His 1,136 direct connections on LinkedIn are connected to 623,300 people. That is over half a million people on LinkedIn that Joe is one introduction away from. If we consider who those people are connected to, the number is almost 13 million people. That is a lot of people (about the population of New York City, Los Angeles, and Chicago combined). Consider for a moment the amount of information and access within a network of 13 million people. Online social networks have revealed to everyone truly how quickly and powerfully networks grow and evolve. Never before has the power of networks been so transparent. Without anyone's permission and without spending any money, we can access millions of people that we are linked to through people that we know. There is vast social capital on the other side of the people that we know.

Power

The second major factor to consider as you think about social capital value is power: how much power does an individual possess? Everyone has power. Some of us use it, some of us do not, but we all have power in varying degrees that comes from a variety of sources. Often when we think of power, we only think of formal types of power. We view people with big titles in big companies as being powerful. We see elected officials as powerful. But this is only one of many types of power. Without an appreciation for what personal power is and where it comes from, we can easily be misguided in our efforts to connect to people. This can lead us to focus all of our attention on the CEO types and to overlook others who have great power to share with us.

Jason's wife Angie is a pastry chef who runs a small business providing dessert catering services. Not long ago, she received a call from a woman to create a small wedding cake for a themed luncheon for about 30 women. Despite the fact that ordering a wedding cake for anything other than a wedding seemed a bit odd, she took the order. She didn't get much other detail about the event. Later, Angie learned that this luncheon had actually been for a group of some of the richest women in Omaha, the kind of women who host lots of parties that can keep a caterer busy. Suddenly, the customer who placed this order became a very important customer to Angie, because she had the power to expose her business to this group of women. So, Angie spent more time fostering that relationship. Power isn't always obvious at first, but is an important factor when thinking about your network.

There is a long and impressive list of people that have driven great change on this planet without being in charge of any formal organization or institution. Gandhi was in charge of nothing. Rosa Parks was in charge of nothing. Wangari Maathai was in charge of nothing when she first introduced her vision of tree planting as community building. On a smaller scale, even the two of us have started or helped to start a variety of positive community initiatives, often without having any formal power. So, take a broad lens toward the idea of power in yourself and in others.

A person can be powerful—and a powerful addition to our network—in a lot of different ways. A little time spent with Google reveals hundreds of ways to define power. In our opinion, one of the best definitions of power comes from Jeffrey Pfeffer of Stanford University:

> **"Power is the potential ability to influence behavior, to change the course of events, to overcome resistance, and to get people to do things that they otherwise would not do."** [12]

If we simplify this definition further, it basically says that if you can influence behavior and overcome resistance, you have power. This kind of power flows from many different sources. To identify sources of power, we can simply inquire into what gives us the ability to influence behavior or overcome resistance. In our work, we teach people to understand and build their own sources of power. Power can be developed, expanded, and lost. By understanding what power is and how it works, we can both cultivate it in ourselves and identify it in others.

Here is a list of some of the most common sources of power:

Formal position: As we have already discussed, formal position is a source of power. We have all seen how a person can influence behavior and overcome resistance simply because of his or her title or formal authority. There are things that your boss can do simply because he or she is your boss. Being "in charge" makes it easier for one to influence behavior and overcome resistance.

Communication skills: The ability to articulate ideas and arguments in ways that others can easily understand and relate to is one of the most underappreciated forms of power. Communications skills range from one-on-one conversation to speaking in front of a group to writing. Politics is an easy example of this. Regardless of what you think of him or his politics, President Barack Obama has powerful communication skills that have played a key role in his ability to overcome resistance and influence behavior, starting with convincing people to vote for him. In national elections especially, we cannot hope to get to know the candidates, so their ability to communicate is a huge part of the equation.

Empathy and sensitivity to the interests of others: Regardless of the actual merit of an idea or initiative, it is more likely to be supported when it considers the interests, priorities, and motivations of others—specifically those who must support it for it to happen. Having the ability to understand the needs and desires of others and their perspective on those ideas is very powerful.

Expertise: Being the expert on a specific topic or discipline gives you power. The more rare the expertise and more difficult that expertise is to develop, the more power that expertise brings. In the medical community, heart and brain surgeons are powerful because there are a limited number of experts in those areas, and gaining that expertise takes years. We have probably all been in situations in which a physician, lawyer, or airline pilot was the most powerful person on hand, simply because of his or her unique expertise in that given situation.

Information access: People within an organization or community that have access to or know where to find valuable information can have great power, because people who need that information must come to them to get it. The more valuable, rare, and hard to attain the information is, the more power that access to this information represents. Most of us had not heard of Julian Assange, the man behind WikiLeaks, before 2010, but he quickly became a person of great interest and power to large corporations, the world of journalism, and even the world's most powerful governments. Julian Assange built a tremendous amount of power because of the information that he had access to and could release at his discretion to the world.

Conflict tolerance and management: Most of us are not good with conflict and generally avoid it. Those who can not only tolerate conflict but also skillfully manage it toward positive outcomes possess a rare sort of power. These people can overcome resistance in situations where most people quit or run away. Thus, they are often able to achieve things that others cannot. One of the things that makes Jo Frost, star of reality television show Supernanny, so good at her job is that she is able to remain focused and level-headed amid family conflict and drama. When the kids are losing their minds and hurling profanity at their parents and their parents are in turn losing their minds, Frost is able to stay focused on effectively resolving the issue in a positive way rather than resorting to an emotional or knee-jerk reaction.

Risk tolerance: Much like conflict tolerance, risk tolerance is another rare source of power. Some people are more willing to take chances. This willingness to step outside of safety and comfort differentiates them from others. Big ideas and change initiatives will usually meet significant resistance. Risk takers don't let this potential resistance stop them from taking action. Do you know people that are willing to experiment, try new things, and take on risk? Do you know people that are early adopters, not necessarily waiting for something to become mainstream? Those people are powerful.

Track record: Having a reputation as someone who gets things done and follows up on commitments is a source of power, mainly because it has to be earned over time. There is no shortcut to a track record. Developing a strong track record is also a critical part of achieving formal power. Those at the top of organizational charts in most companies are people who have a history of producing results and getting things done.

Focus: The ability to remain focused and clear on your objectives and not get distracted is a source of power. Along the process of any major change, many challenges will arise, and resistance will come up. It is easy to become distracted along the way, and most people do. The ability to stay laser focused on the end result, in spite of these distractions, is a source of power.

This list is not an exhaustive list of sources of power, but it highlights some of the most common. As you think about these sources of power, take a look at your network of connections and consider how much power exists within it. Every member of your network has power. The framework we have shared here is simply a framework for understanding what that power might be. It's likely that as you think about your network using the power lens, you will notice that there are areas where your network—and, as a result, your social capital—is lacking power. Use these realizations to seek out new connections who add value in those areas.

Diversity

The final factor to consider as you think about social capital value is diversity. Diversity (or difference) is an incredibly robust dynamic within networks of relationships. Without some appreciation for the difference that difference makes, your efforts to build social capital can be seriously handicapped. Step number one is probably to throw out everything that you have been told regarding diversity. This is not a conversation about race relations, the significance of gender in 21st-century America, institutional bias, or the true meaning of social justice. Those are all important conversations, but they will happen in a different place. This is a conversation about the dynamics and the value of difference and what difference can mean for your network.

Difference is a powerful ingredient that exists in every interaction between human beings. Difference can take many forms, including differences in our social identities (race, gender, age, etc.), differences in our cognitive orientations (thinking styles), and behavioral and affective differences. We are all different from each other, so diversity is present in all of our relationships. Every new connection that we make brings some amount of difference into our networks, but, left to our own devices, we generally minimize the difference that we integrate.

We have a strong tendency as human beings to feel most comfortable around those that we think are like us. So, it is not uncommon for our personal and professional networks to be heavily populated by people who have a lot of things in common with us. To build powerful social capital, we have to push back on this tendency, because embracing only those who are most like us is very limiting. Diversity in our network of connections is actually a "force multiplier." If you and I both have 100 connections, but you have substantially more diversity in your network than I do, you are likely to have greater social capital. By having more diversity in your network, you place yourself at a more unique and more robust intersection of thoughts, ideas, professions, cultures, disciplines, and so on. This diversity provides the opportunity to synthesize and pull from a broader range of information, experiences, and perspectives.

In The Social Origin of Good Ideas, Ronald Burt demonstrates that diversity in a person's network of relationships can enhance his or her ability to drive innovation and creative problem solving. He looked at the number of ideas and quality of ideas contributed by employees within a large company over a number of years, and there was one correlation. The people who had relationships with colleagues from across the organization submitted more ideas, and they submitted better ideas. Those who had relationships with people primarily within their "silo" were less likely to submit ideas and less likely to submit high-quality ideas. You can actually make yourself a more robust portal for ideas and solutions by putting yourself at more unique intersections through your connections.

Putting yourself at a busy intersection of different perspectives also makes you less susceptible to groupthink and conformity, which, while very safe and comfortable in the short term, are deadly to you and your organization in the long term.

For the authors, diversity continues to show up in our networks of relationships simply through having worked in different roles in different industries. Joe has served in the Marine Corps, has worked in nonprofit and for-profit organizations, and has connections to people from those worlds, which are in some ways very different. Jason has a network that is reflective of years in sales, recruiting, management, and HR leadership, in addition to a great deal of volunteer work with and for very different kinds of organizations.

Think of your network of relationships as a container. Think of it as a large stew pot. Think of the individual relationships that you have as the ingredients you put into the pot. The more variety you have in your ingredients, the greater potential that you have to create something new. The greater the amount of diversity in your relationships, the more powerful your network will be.

You may really like pinto beans. You may even love pinto beans. But a stew consisting of only pinto beans would be boring at best and terrible at worst. If you had a stew of only pinto beans, each additional pinto bean has little marginal value to the stew, as it is just one more of what you already have. The new bean adds only to how much stew you have, not to the quality, flavor, or complexity of the stew. Nothing new is really being added. The stew is still boring.

Let's look at a more tangible example. If you had four close friends and they all happened to be accountants working and living in Omaha, there would likely be a great deal of overlap in their information, perspectives, and experiences. They each would be different from each other in some way, but these four individuals would have a great many things in common. Alternately, if you had four close friends that all worked in different professions and lived in different parts of the country, they would probably have far less in common with each other than the four accountants from Omaha. Therefore, they would create a network consisting of a much broader collection of ideas, perspectives, and experiences.

Connections are in some ways like lottery tickets. If you were to buy just one lottery ticket, you might be very intentional about the number on that ticket. The number you select might consist of your lucky number, your ex-lover's phone number, your child's date of birth, or some other meaningful number. If you were to just play one ticket, you would use your most lucky, most special, most favorite number. Regardless of how much you believed in the magic of that particular number, if you were to purchase a second ticket, you would not want it to have the same number as the first ticket, because a second ticket with the same number doesn't increase your odds of winning. It adds to the number of tickets that you have but not to the quality of your chance of winning. We want diversity in the numbers we choose on multiple lottery tickets, because that diversity of numbers increases the likelihood of winning. When it comes to playing the lottery, we have an intuitive grasp on the significance of diversity. If we play two tickets or

1,000 tickets, we all know that diversity among tickets increases our probability of winning. This is the difference that difference makes.

You can also increase the value of your network by intentionally seeking out difference. Those four accountants in Omaha are probably great people to know, and we don't suggesting that you end your relationship with them or avoid them. But, by seeking out and adding people to your network from different geographies, professions, education levels, socioeconomic status, professional status, race, gender, and so on, you can add additional dimensions and power to your network.

Just like you, each person you connect with has a personal network that provides him or her with information as well. When you connect to acquaintances who occupy different physical, social, cultural, or professional spaces than you do, you establish a pipeline to new information. A person who lives in a different area of town may know about events, shops, or places to go that you may never have discovered on your own. While you might not be personally plugged into the art scene in your city, adding acquaintances who are might lead to invitations to great cultural events that you would have missed in the past. Actively seeking out and connecting to people outside of your group of friends will open the door to new ideas and connections.

The Choice

Now that we have shared this framework with you for evaluating the value of connections in your network, we also have to leave the choice firmly in your hands. Value means different things to different people. We believe the three factors we have presented are the most critical to amassing the social capital riches to drive your external success. But, there are many reasons for relationships that span beyond these boundaries. There are people you know who make you laugh. That may be the one thing they bring to your life, and that might be incredibly important to you. Our message in this chapter is not intended to suggest that people like this don't add value. Rather, we suggest that you think intentionally about all of the people who you put and keep in your network. If you recall, Dunbar's research says that there are only about

150 spots we can each fill with people and keep active relationships with. Make sure that those 150 spots are filled with people who bring value to your life and fuel your future success. Our framework is not meant to replace your personal judgment, intuition, and common sense. When the two of us met, we probably did not offer much to each other in the way of reach, diversity, or power, but we became good friends and we eventually became collaborators on a variety of projects.

Harnessing Social Gravity

Spend time analyzing your network for reach, power, and diversity.

1. Who in your network has the greatest reach?

_____

- How are you building overlap with these people?

_____

2. In what types of power is your network the strongest?

_____

- Who is contributing the most to this power?

_____

- How are you building overlap with these people?

_____

3. In what types of power is your network lacking?

_____

- How might you increase that power?

_____

4. How diverse is your network?

_____

- What can you do to increase its diversity?

_____

CHAPTER 5:

THIS IS YOUR NETWORK ON TECHNOLOGY

A survey of books written prior to 2000 about networking and building relationships will emphasize the skills necessary to make good first impressions and business relationships in person. Today, we live in a digital world where the rules of engagement have evolved. The Rolodex has been replaced by online contact-management systems like Outlook. In most cases, handwritten notes have been replaced by email. Direct-mail marketing has been replaced by electronic newsletters. Beyond that, the internet has brought the world together and made it almost easier to make a new connection in India than one across the street. The importance of in-person, face-to-face relationship building will never go away, but we cannot deny the fact that technology has dramatically changed how connections are made and how people keep in touch. In this chapter, we will explore the implications of the changes wrought by technology, specifically social media, on the creation and management of social capital.

What is Social Media?

Terms such as social media, social networking, and Web 2.0 have all lost a great deal of their meaning as the lines between social media and social networks have become blurry. When we use the phrase social media, we are talking about online tools and platforms that are relational in nature. That means that they allow you to interact with other human beings. To understand the difference between traditional media and social media, let's consider two examples, a magazine and an online blog. A magazine is a traditional type of media and is not an example of social media because it represents a one-way interaction. The publishers of the magazine write, and you read. There is no interaction between people with or around a magazine. In contrast, an online blog is an example of social media because it allows for readers to post comments and interact directly with the author of the post and other readers. Because people are interacting both with each other and around the blog, it's considered to be a form of social media.

Social media has exploded into our lives, and it is changing things dramatically. Social networks that did not exist 10 years ago have hundreds of millions of users today and are growing fast. Applications that did not exist five years ago now have millions of passionate users. We have an affinity as humans for connection with each other, and social media makes it easier than ever. This affinity is clearly a powerful drive, and we are rapidly embracing tools that empower us and support us in our efforts to seek it out.

After its launch in 2002, one of the first social networking sites to experience great popularity was Friendster. It was a site that made it easy for us to find people with similar interests, share information with each other, and express ourselves publicly. Following that success, we have seen the continued evolution and growing popularity of sites such as MySpace, Facebook, and LinkedIn, and new hybrid sites such as SecondLife, FriendFeed, Ning, YouTube, Flickr, and Twitter. These sites incorporate social networking and community building with other forms of communication, sharing, and interaction. Even retail sites such as Amazon and eBay have increasingly incorporated characteristics of social networks.

Rather than spending too much more time exploring the history of social media, what it is, and how to use it (there are many books already written on that topic), we will instead explore the implications of social media on the creation and maintenance of social capital. We'll also share some ideas on how you can leverage these new tools in your efforts to become social capital rich.

Redefining Proximity

As you will recall, physical proximity has been shown to be the most powerful predictor of who we form close relationships with. Before the web, our ability to be in proximity to any person or group was limited to the physical. Social media has given birth to huge numbers of groups, forums, online cliques, and other formal collections of people with common interests. These online communities offer tremendous opportunities to get in proximity to groups of people that we'd like to add to our network.

Proximity in an online world works differently than it does in the physical world. When you and I are neighbors or we sit next to each other at work, we see each other frequently due to our physical proximity. By seeing each other, we acknowledge each other's existence. Every time this happens, we have the opportunity to interact and create overlap between the two of us. This is how close relationships take shape.

In the online community, just joining a group doesn't accomplish much, because the other members of the group cannot "see" you in the way that someone sitting next to you can. So, in the online world, you have to make yourself "seen." This can happen in many ways. One mistake many people make with social media and social networking is that they assume that signing up is enough. Signing up is a required first step, but it doesn't get you seen. Remember that social media is relational; it is designed for people to interact with one another. That interaction in social media has to start with you. Nearly every social media site now provides the opportunity to share short updates with your network. Every time you share an update, you create an opportunity to be seen. The more you are seen, the more opportunity there is for connection with others in your network. Every time you are seen in social media, you create overlap with the people who see you, particularly if your updates share information that helps them learn more about you.

In addition to updates, you can make yourself seen online by joining forums and discussion groups on topics related to your profession or interests. Once you join these groups, the way to make yourself seen is by posting questions to the group, responding to the questions posted by others, and generally participating in the group's online activities. This has the same effect as posting updates to your profile. Every time you post something, you create the opportunity to be seen by others within the group. Chances are, if you have joined the right groups, these are people who you'd like to add to your network.

By the time you read this book, social media will probably have evolved even further. It's likely that some new, exciting site will have emerged where you can go to interact. The important thing to remember, regardless of what site you choose to engage with, is that signing up isn't enough. You have to make a commitment to interact with others. By interacting, you put proximity to work in your favor in an entirely new way.

CONNECTED JOE

On March 6, 2008, I signed up on Twitter. I am not sure why I signed up. Twitter did not make a lot of sense to me, and that did not change for the first few weeks. The site did not even work very reliably in those days, and in retrospect I am surprised that I actually kept using it. But something about Twitter kept me coming back, and I began to connect to some people. One of the first people I met on Twitter was Maren Hogan. The funny thing about meeting Maren on Twitter was that she actually lives within walking distance of my house, but we had never met.

Maren and I had some common interests, and we chatted regularly on Twitter. Eventually, we had coffee and became friends. As Maren and I got to know each other, she suggested I talk to one of her friends named Susan. I connected to Susan on Twitter, and we eventually scheduled the first of many phone calls. It turned out that Susan and I also had a lot in common, and our conversations generally covered a broad range of topics. I think that we both knew after our first phone conversation that we

would probably end up collaborating on something. I also learned that Susan was a frequent traveler. So, when I was planning a trip with my wife, I asked Susan for a recommendation. Susan suggested that we try Sanibel and Captiva Islands on the West coast of Florida. In February 2009, my wife and I enjoyed the big beautiful beaches of Sanibel and Captiva. We took her suggestion and had an amazing trip.

Susan is also the executive director of the Future of Talent Institute. Her organization provides thought leadership to their corporate members through white papers and webinars. At one point, Susan invited me to write a white paper and facilitate a webinar on diversity and inclusion for her members. It was my first white paper and webinar, so it was a big deal to me. As a result of doing this webinar and white paper, I ended up with a great new client in Southern California who had been looking for someone to bring an actionable message regarding diversity and inclusion to their emerging-leaders program.

This is the power of social media. New friends, new business, and visits to both coasts that would not have happened had I not been willing to experiment with Twitter.

The Small World Effect

Since social media knows no geographic boundaries, it's easier now than ever to be in proximity to people around the world, creating the opportunity for our networks to expand dramatically. Social media is in effect making a small world even smaller. It is now fairly easy to find and interact with someone in another part of the country or even the planet because of the internet and the applications that facilitate that connectivity. We can connect to others who share a common interest by publishing a blog about that topic or contributing to others' blogs. We can connect to others in our profession or our geography easily, because this information is a common part of social networking profiles. Thanks to social media, we can maintain a larger number of connections than ever before, and these connections can have a tremendous geographic and cultural diversity.

The underlying impact of all of these points is that social media has crushed traditional limitations to building a global network. With some intentional effort and focus, there is nothing to prevent a motivated individual from building global social capital. If you can get a high-speed internet connection and a computer, you have all the tools you need to make it happen.

The Brand Called You

In the past few years, there has been an explosion of books and seminars on the topic of "personal branding." Most of this has been fueled by the rise of social media. While the concept of branding has existed for decades, the idea of extending this kind of discipline to the individual is relatively new. For the definition of personal brand, we turn to one of the experts in the field, Dan Schawbel, the author of *Me 2.0: Build a Powerful Brand to Achieve Career Success*:

> **Personal branding describes the process by which individuals and entrepreneurs differentiate themselves and stand out from a crowd by identifying and articulating their unique value proposition, whether professional or personal, and then leveraging it across platforms with a consistent message and image to achieve a specific goal. In this way, individuals can enhance their recognition as experts in their field, establish reputation and credibility, advance their careers, and build self-confidence.[13]**

One of the really powerful effects of social media we've already discussed is that it makes it easy to find other people with whom you'd like to connect. At the same time, it makes you easier to find, as well. This is where personal branding comes into the discussion. Developing your personal brand is about making some decisions to define how you package who you are for the online community and to help the right people find you online. A well-defined brand will draw people into your network who you want to connect with. This is not an easy process, but it is incredibly important for those who are serious about building social capital.

To emphasize further the importance of personal branding, we turn to the clever networking book Guerilla Networking by Monroe Mann and Jay Conrad Levinson. In this book, these two master networkers put forth the simple idea that great networking isn't simply about meeting people but rather that it's about becoming a person that other people want to meet. While this idea may be new to many of us, it makes sense. It's much easier and more comfortable to meet new people when they already want to meet you. Done effectively, this approach can be very fruitful and can take much of the anxiety out of making new connections. While they don't specifically tie the concept back to brand building in their book, it's hard to deny that the two ideas are certainly linked.

So, what does it mean to have a personal brand? Personal branding is a process of determining the impression you desire to make on the world around you. A brand is a formal way of presenting who you are and what you stand for. While most of our discussion in this chapter has been about the online world, a personal brand lives in every interaction of your life. Ultimately, a personal brand impacts how you act, look, and sound.

For example, if your career goals include being a corporate executive in the future, you may decide that a part of your personal brand is to be viewed as a consummate professional. To "live" this brand, you would probably make choices like acting professionally at all times. If you attend a social event, even with friends, you may choose not to be the drunkest, craziest person at the party because of your desire to be viewed as professional. You may also choose to invest more money in your professional wardrobe or to have all of your clothes professionally tailored and dry-cleaned. As for how you sound, you would probably choose to write and speak more formally than others around you. It might also be an intentional choice for you to refrain from using profanity and slang when you speak. All of these actions could be viewed as part of building and developing your personal brand as a consummate professional. Consider how all of these decisions might be different if your personal brand was as a rock and roll musician or an exercise and nutrition expert. That's personal brand.

This personal brand becomes very important as you begin to establish your online identity. Returning to our example, if you're brand is a consummate professional, you'd probably want to look into having a professional photograph taken to use in your online profiles. In these photos, you'd wear clothing and groom yourself in a way that projects a professional image. The language you use when corresponding online should reflect your brand as well. These are the basics of how a personal brand works online.

If you are serious about developing a robust personal brand, it requires a commitment of time and effort to do it well. You may not have the time to invest in a major personal branding project right away, but that doesn't mean that you can't get started. Later in this book, we will share with you some steps you can take to get clear on some important pieces that make up your brand, including the development of a personal "manifesto." Clarifying these basic pieces will serve as a great foundation for your brand.

As you bring more clarity to who you are (i.e. what is your personal brand) and who you want to connect to, social media provides incredible opportunities to employ the guerilla networking tactics to become someone who others want to meet. For example, there is no cost to create a blog and begin writing to establish your voice in a particular industry or on a specific topic that relates to your brand. If you have a laptop or $100 to buy a video camera, you can create videos and freely post them to YouTube and elsewhere. You can then establish free accounts on all of the major social networking platforms to promote this content and be seen by those who are interested in the kinds of things you talk or write about. In essence, the cost barrier to become an online celebrity is almost zero. It's just a matter of focus and dedication to define your brand and doing the work to get it out there.

Harnessing Social Gravity

Rate your social media savvy:

☐ Don't have a clue

☐ In the game, but not really doing anything.

☐ In the game, but don't have a game plan.

☐ Winning the game.

Identify social media tools where you can connect to those who would add to your network, establish profiles, join discussions and make a goal to "be seen" at least once per week.

_____

_____

_____

_____

_____

Write down some notes about your personal brand. Is it clear? What about your brand can you emphasize to become a person who others want to meet? How can you emphasize that in your social media efforts?

_____

_____

_____

_____

_____

Section 2

DISCOVER THE LAWS OF SOCIAL GRAVITY

In Section 1, our goal was to demystify the power of social gravity and illustrate its importance. We defined social capital, revealed how it works and examined some of the reasons why it is important. You probably came to this book knowing that relationships with other people are important—you have felt the pull of social gravity in your life. We hope you have now arrived at a grander conclusion. Not only are our relationships with other people important, but these relationships are also the key to our success in all aspects of our lives. Having the right relationship with the right person could be the key to finding your dream job or your future spouse. Social gravity holds the power to help you attract tremendous opportunity into your life if you choose to harness and use it.

With this new perspective, we can start to think about how to position ourselves to benefit from these dynamics. What specific actions must we take to harness the power of social gravity?

In the previous chapters, we've deconstructed social gravity to examine what it looks like and where it comes from.

- Social capital consists of the resources available to us through your relationships, and it can take on many forms, from job leads to movie reviews. Social capital value can come from anything that adds meaning and value to your life.

- Your closest friendships hold value, but another kind of value comes from your acquaintances, or weak ties. The greater the reach, diversity, and power in your network of acquaintances, the greater your social capital.

- While we often think that we seek out relationships with those who share our values and interests, the truth is that physical proximity plays the biggest role in predicting the people who will become your closest offline relationships and connections.

- Networks are exponential. The numbers get big really fast, and social media tools have made this effect more transparent and powerful than ever before.

- Social media is an enormously powerful tool in networking and building social capital. Social media tools have shrunk the world and made it possible to put the forces of proximity to work with people around the globe.

- Social media has amplified the importance of having a well-developed personal brand.

In Section 2 of this book, we change our focus to providing you with the mindset and approaches you need to begin harnessing social gravity. You will learn how to build the connections required to achieve the social capital that will fuel your personal and professional success. This mindset and approach are presented to you as the Six Laws of Social Gravity.

The Six Laws of Social Gravity

1 First Law: Invest in Connecting

2 Second Law: Be Open to Connections

3 Third Law: Be Authentic

4 Fourth Law: Get Involved in Meaningful Activity

5 Fifth Law: Use Karma as a Turbocharger

6 Sixth Law: Stay in Touch

While we'd love to report that we discovered these six laws carved in a marble tablet in the tomb of some ancient king while on a great adventure involving numerous sword fights and brushes with death, the truth is less sexy but far more important. These laws have emerged from two sources: research and experience. We both spent the early part of our careers in sales jobs. A salesperson's success is linked to his or her ability to quickly establish connections and relationships. It was at this point in our lives that we first began to consider the power of relationships, because our paychecks depended on it. While we didn't always have the terminology of "social gravity," we have been studying connections and relationships for most of our adult lives. Our early studies consisted primarily of sales trainings (the good, the bad, and the ugly) and reading of the classic Dale Carnegie book, How to Win Friends and Influence People. Our studies and reading have grown and evolved from there.

More important than our study of this topic is our experience. Perhaps it was our early exploits in sales or perhaps it was just our personalities, but we've both been networking and leveraging the relationships in our lives for as long as we can remember. Even as young professionals, we were often asked, "How do you know everyone?" Certainly, we didn't know everyone and never will, but because we understood how to harness the power of social gravity, it appeared to others that we did. This question ultimately became the catalyst that led to this book.

The six laws are not magical. We have extracted from our collective knowledge and experience six key ideas that we believe are central to establishing the social capital you need to unlock the power of social gravity in your life. Our goal was to break down the process into its key parts and to help you understand not only what to do but also why each step is important.

It may seem presumptuous to you that we call our six discoveries "laws." We chose to use "law" not for the jurisprudential definition (you will not be given a ticket or put in jail if you break these laws) but rather invoke the idea found in the laws of nature. The law of gravity, for example, was not written into existence. It was discovered by a brilliant scientist, Sir Isaac Newton. He did not create gravity; he discovered its existence and described it to others so that they could take that new understanding and leverage it in their own pursuits. Regardless of your agreement or disagreement with the law of gravity, gravity exists. If you drop an apple, it will fall to the ground. It is in this same vein that we have chosen to incorporate the power of the word "law" to describe social gravity. Clearly, we didn't write these laws into existence. Instead, our work has revealed them to us. And, like the law of gravity, regardless of your agreement with them, they exist and play a role in your life every day.

These laws apply to everyone at every stage in life. Armed with an awareness of these laws, you can make more well-informed decisions and take action regarding your network of relationships. If you follow these laws, your social capital will grow. As it does, you will see great things happen throughout your life. This is true regardless of your title, age, profession, or how many people you know right now.

Behold, the Six Laws of Social Gravity.

CHAPTER 6:

FIRST LAW: INVEST IN CONNECTING

CONNECTED JASON

Many years ago, I was a young entrepreneur working to get a newly formed recruiting business up and running. As a small-business owner, my main job was to make connections that could lead to new business for the company. This led me to be continually on the lookout for any chance to do some networking with other business leaders in the community. At the time, the local chamber of commerce was launching a new event called Business on the Green, which was basically a networking event on the golf course. Since I like to golf, I jumped at the opportunity to mix business with pleasure. The event was set up for people to register and be randomly put together with three others professionals to play a round of golf.

In my foursome that day was a man named Chris with whom I shared my golf cart. During the course of the golf outing that day, Chris and I both played some of the worst golf ever seen. Thankfully for Chris and me, they had given us drink tickets, so we drowned our golfing woes in several beers. The positive side effect of playing horrible golf was the bonding experience it presented to Chris and me. We became friends that day, and, as we parted ways that evening, we exchanged information and agreed to keep in touch (which we did).

It wasn't until about five years later that the potential power of my connection with Chris was revealed. I had spent those years as an entrepreneur and had decided it was time to go back to work for corporate America to collect a regular paycheck for a while. So, I was in the market for a new job. I recalled that Chris had told me about the company he worked for, and it seemed from his description that he really liked working there. I was looking for a human resources management position, so I called Chris and asked if he would be willing to introduce me to the vice president of human resources at his organization. He honored my request and thanks to his introduction, I met with that VP (her name was Mary) within the week. As luck would have it, they were in the market for a new manager in their HR department.

Here's where the story gets really interesting. While I was in the interviewing process with Mary and others at the company, she brought up my name over dinner one night with her husband (as part of the normal "how was your day?" conversation). Mary's husband's name is Joe. I hadn't realized it yet, but I also knew Joe. Joe and I had met through a networking event years ago, and we periodically got together for coffee to share leads and ideas with one another. Upon hearing that she was interviewing me for a role on her team, Joe gave me an emphatic endorsement that played heavily into Mary's ultimate decision to hire me.

The moral of this story is that I was hired for a great job not due to my resume alone or my brilliant interviewing skills; rather, it was my relationships with Chris and Joe that made all of the difference. Had I not invested the time in building relationships with Chris and Joe, I would have missed out on a great opportunity.

> "Today is the day to invest in those people we hope will call us 'old friends' in the years to come."
>
> – Grant Fairley

The actions we take today will have consequences for the future. This is a lesson bestowed upon us throughout our lives. If we don't study hard in school, we won't get into a good college after we graduate. If we don't go to college, our job opportunities will be limited down the road. If we smoke today, we will likely get cancer in the future. If you don't start saving for retirement early, you won't have enough money to live on when your time to retire comes. The list goes on.

It's when we take ownership as individuals for these consequences that we open up great potential for success. Taking ownership means embracing that each action you take has the potential to positively or negatively impact your future. Each action wisely chosen is an investment in your future success. As a motivated person who wants to do everything possible to succeed, making the most of each day and each opportunity is paramount.

Take a second to think of the most successful people you know. Would you describe any of those people as lazy? Probably not. If you are reading this book, you likely have some appreciation for the fact that success takes work. It requires that we go beyond what's easy or comfortable. Each of us has the potential to be wildly successful, whether we define success in terms of professional, financial, academic, civic, artistic, or other accomplishment. The question is not one of potential or talent but of the will to make the required investment to make it happen.

Warren Buffett is famous for his investment and business success. If you peek into Buffett's history, you will discover that he has spent his life making not only financial investments but also other sorts of investments in himself as early as age 10. At this early age, he was already spending some of his free time hanging out in the customer lounge of the offices of a regional stock brokerage near his father's office to be around those who invested their money regularly. He also insisted that his family visit the New York Stock Exchange on a vacation to New York City that same year. At age 11, he bought his first stocks. When it came time a few years later to select a graduate school, he chose to attend the university where Benjamin Graham was a professor. Graham was the author of Buffett's favorite book on investing, and he would end up playing an important role in Buffett's future. It would be hard to argue that Warren Buffett didn't have some natural talent for business. But, it is also clear that an important part of Buffett's success was investing his time and energy very intentionally to build his knowledge, skill, and network to fuel his future success.[14]

Financially successful people become that way because they are experts at investing. Some people have expertise in investing money in the stock market. Others are experts at investing their time and talent in creation of business opportunities. Others are experts at investing in a powerful network of connections with other people. Regardless of what successful person you study, each will have mastered the ability to invest time, focus, and resources in the right things to fuel success.

Investment 101

To become skilled in investing, you need the right mindset and a plan. There are many different approaches to investing money to create wealth, but most experts generally agree on a few common principles that they recommend everyone follow.[15] These principles can be best summarized as:

1. Define your goals.
2. Leverage the power of compounding.
3. Embrace the long-term approach.

The first piece of advice is to define your goals. In other words, get clear on why you are investing. Are you saving for retirement, the kids' college fund, or to buy a new boat? All of these are legitimate reasons to save, but each would entail a different investment strategy. Without getting clear on this goal up front, it's difficult to choose the right strategy.

The second piece of advice is to leverage the power of compounding for financial investments. Compounding in financial investments is defined as the ability of an asset to generate earnings, which are then reinvested in order to generate their own earnings.[16] Basically, if you invest money well, it will earn you interest. If you then invest that interest well, it can earn interest and so on. By making wise investments over time of both your initial investment and the interest it earns, your money can grow exponentially.

The final piece of investment advice is to embrace the long-term view of investing. According to one expert, "We believe the best approach to investing is the long-term one. Pick your investments well and you'll reap greater rewards over the long term than you had ever dreamed possible."[17] This seems to suggest that there isn't a reliable shortcut in investing that will lead to great riches. Instead, you must adopt a mindset to do the right things repeatedly over time and have the patience to allow those decisions to work to your advantage.

This advice is great advice for investing money, but it also serves as a good framework when you think about how to invest your time and energy in growing your social capital. Each of these three concepts has direct application to building the connections with other people that will unlock great wealth in all aspects of your life.

Know Your Goals

CONNECTED JOE

In early 2008, I joined Twitter. I'll admit that at first, I didn't really understand what it was or how it worked. I had been plugging away as a consulting company of one and was increasingly interested in easy and cheap ways to introduce myself and my work to more people, especially people outside of my immediate geography. It seemed that Twitter was a tool that could potentially help me do that, so I decided to invest some serious effort in using it.

I spent many hours on Twitter connecting with people and developing relationships. Many of these relationships eventually grew beyond Twitter. One of the ways I used Twitter was to find people who were interested in diversity and inclusion, the focus of my work. But, I also tried to connect to a variety of people from across the country and the world. One of the people that I interacted with quite a bit in

that first year on Twitter reached out to me one day about a conference she was planning in Virginia. It was going to be the first conference in that area specific to the implications and opportunities associated with social media. She had been impressed with how I used Twitter, so she asked if I would be the keynote speaker for this event. I had never done a keynote presentation at a conference, so this was a pretty big deal for me. Shortly after, I landed another conference engagement through a Twitter connection for my largest speaking fee to that point.

So, let's recap. I had a goal to expand my network to help grow my business. Twitter looked like a good way to build connections nationally, so despite not being sure exactly what would come of it, I invested some time to learn how to make Twitter work for me. As a result, I had landed both my first keynote speaking engagement and to that point my highest-paid speaking gig. Turns out, Twitter was a good investment for me.

When we talk about investing in the creation of social capital, what are we investing? In this case, it's not money, at least not directly. We can't go out and buy an authentic network of connections. Instead, what we are really investing is time, effort, and attention. Connecting with others takes time. Creating overlap with those connections to develop relationships takes time. And time is at a premium. Similar to money, we have many ways that we can spend our time. Investing money generally means making a decision to take some money that could have been spent on something more immediate and put it instead into something that will hopefully bring rewards down the road. The same is true for investing time. You could spend two hours watching television, or you could invest that time at a business networking event or having dinner with an acquaintance. Each day, we make decisions on how to invest our time, and those decisions show up in the returns that we get in our lives.

Since time is the major resource required to build social capital, the way you use time is critically important to your success. Time management is a popular and widely written-about set of skills. If you need to learn the skills of time management, there are plenty of other books that cover that topic in great detail, so we won't go into it here. However, there is one framework from the discipline of time management that is particularly relevant when it comes to making decisions about how to invest your time in growing your social capital.

This particular approach involves thinking about the possible ways you can spend your time in terms of their urgency and their importance. Urgent items are those that require immediate attention because they are time sensitive. Responding to emails or returning phone calls are generally considered to be urgent items because the person on the other end of that correspondence is expecting your reply. Importance, on the other hand, speaks to the significance of an activity related to achieving your goals. If you have a goal to get in great physical shape, working out daily is probably an important activity for you. The power in this approach is that all of your actions and potential actions can be evaluated on both their urgency and their importance relative to the other options available to you. Stephen Covey famously presented this concept visually as the "time management matrix" we show below.[18] This matrix encourages you to categorize all of your activities into one of four quadrants: Urgent and

Important, Urgent and Not Important, Not Urgent and Important, and Not Urgent and Not Important.

	Urgent	Not Urgent
Important	**Quadrant I:** • crisis • pressing problems • deadline-driven projects	**Quadrant II:** • prevention • relationship building • planning
Not Important	**Quadrant III:** • interruptions • phone calls • meetings • emails	**Quadrant IV:** • trivia • busy work • some email • some phone calls

When you consider the matrix, it becomes clear that the most important and valuable way to use your time is on the activities found in Quadrants I and II, the items of importance to you. Of course you want to pursue things that are important. Not only are the activities in Quadrant II important, but they are things that don't have any major consequences for not taking immediate action. While it probably seems obvious that it's important to focus your energy on the activities in this quadrant, it is far easier said than done. Urgent activities, like checking email or watching the latest episode of your favorite TV show, are very seductive, and they will tend to dominate your time unless you are intentional and disciplined about managing your time.

Many years ago, a human resources manager named Mike learned the importance of investing in social capital before it becomes urgent to do so. Mike told us a story of how he was the guy who was too busy to network. He didn't belong to any networking or professional groups. He didn't accept or return phone calls from people he didn't know. And, he certainly didn't go out of his way to meet new people. He was just too busy with his work and his life, so networking was never a priority for him. But, the events of one day changed his perspective on the importance of having a network. On that day, his job was suddenly eliminated as a part of a "reduction in force" at his corporate employer. Mike, like most people, didn't expect this to ever happen to him. So, he was completely unprepared to find himself as part of a very competitive job market. It was at this moment of his life that he realized he had no network to call on for help. He suddenly needed a network urgently, and he had to start from scratch. He discovered how difficult it is to establish a valuable network in a hurry. Mike now knows the significance of investing in social capital long before you need it. He has never forgotten that experience and has since committed significant time and energy connecting with others and sharing his story so they don't have to learn this lesson as painfully as he did.

To put the urgent-important approach to work, we must ensure we know what's important in our lives and careers. We need to spend some time thinking about why we want to invest in social capital. We need to have some goals. As with financial investing, you can have multiple reasons for wanting to invest in social capital. Examples of these goals might be:

- Grow your consulting business.
- Make a sale to that new customer you've been pursuing for a long time.
- Earn a promotion or just do your current job more effectively.
- Be "in the know" about what's happening in your organization or community.

Take time to write these goals down now. You probably have several goals. Each goal helps provide clarity for how you might approach building your social capital. For example, if my primary goal is to get promoted in the next year, I'd likely invest my time building relationships internally within my company. This might mean that I would prioritize my time to spend more of it with my coworkers and peers than at an external Chamber of Commerce networking event. Alternatively, if I was trying to start or grow my own small business, it would be the opposite. Getting clear on your goals will help you both to establish priorities and to determine what is important. This will help you focus on why you are investing time and energy into building social capital in the first place.

My Most Important Goals

1._____

2._____

3._____

4._____

5._____

The Power of Compounding

When you invest your money wisely, it earns interest and your money grows. If you then invest your interest wisely, it begins to earn interest, and the rate at which your money grows increases faster. This effect is called compounding. This is the reason that we are told as young adults to invest as much as we can early on, because one dollar invested today turns into a lot of dollars over 40 years due to compounding.

Your network of connections has a similar compounding effect. Each person who you connect to has a network of relationships in his or her personal and professional life. By establishing a meaningful connection with that person, you are now one introduction away from this new network of potential connections. Over time, even without any intentional effort to grow a network, your number of connections increases. You change jobs or departments (new coworkers), you buy a house (new neighbors), and your friends and relatives get married (new spouses). By simply living life, your connections grow over time. So, the compounding impact of social capital boils down to math.

Let's assume that today you have 20 connections and each of them also has 20 connections. If you do the math, you find that you are one introduction away from 400 people.

Your 20 connections X their 20 connections =
400 potential connections

Now, let's assume that over the next five years, you maintain your 20 connections and you add 10 new connections in the normal course of life. Let's also assume that each of your connections has done the same. Now the math looks like this:

Your 30 connections X their 30 connections =
900 potential connections

By adding 10 new connections (increasing your network by 50 percent), you have increased the potential introductions available to you by 500 (or 125 percent). That's a pretty impressive growth in your network of connections. This is the compounding effect of building connections. Just like your 401K, the earlier you start investing time in building connections, the greater the social capital you will have in the long run.

In addition to compounding in numbers, your connections also compound in value. It is natural for most people to follow a career path that leads to increasingly more significant positions of power or influence. For some, this progression happens because they are talented and ambitious. For others, it's due to diligent and loyal service to an organization over decades. The point is that someone who may not have much formal power within his or her organization or community today may have significant power in years to come. These connections established today will continue to grow in terms of value and influence over time, making each of the growing number of connections in your network increasingly valuable.

One of the first conference speaking engagements Joe had as an independent consultant was at a Nebraska conference on community service. His consulting business was only a few months old, so any opportunity to get in front of an audience to show his stuff was a good one, even if it wasn't compensated. In the audience at that event was Pippi Van Slooten. At the end of Joe's session that day, Pippi approached him to ask for his business card and compliment him on the presentation. As it turns out, Pippi worked in city government, and she hired Joe to do a workshop for her staff. The workshop was a hit. This led to Pippi and her coworkers to hire Joe as a keynote speaker for a conference they were planning. Again, Joe's presentation was well received, and that ultimately led to some new connections and to another keynote speaking opportunity at a different conference. Like the others, this one too led to yet another keynote opportunity. This is the power of compounding in social capital. One relationship with Pippi Van Slooten developed over time into significant new connections that each led to profitable work for Joe's business.

Take the Long-Term Approach

As we discussed earlier, most people get serious about networking when they need a network. Sticking to our financial example, if I don't know how to invest and don't have a lot of money to invest today, the chances of my becoming rich by next week are slim to none. You might start earning a small amount of interest right away, but the accumulation of significant wealth takes years.

There are no reliable shortcuts to investment success. Granted, there are exceptions to every rule (we like to call them flukes), and we have all heard the stories about the stock that went from $5 a share to $50 a share in 12 months. Those investments are few and far between. The reality is that an investor looking for the short-term payout is going to invest in a lot of stocks that fail before finding the one the pays off big, if ever finding it at all. The better strategy, as we learned earlier, is to take a long-term approach and trust that making wise investment decisions will pay off over time.

This long-term approach applies to social capital as well. Since social capital is the outcome of your connections and relationships with others, the true value of social capital reveals itself over time. As we talked about in the Chapter 3, the more overlap you create in relationships, the more value will be revealed. Creating overlap takes time. It's also true that networks evolve, grow, and change over time. As an example, someone you know today could be the person who will introduce you to your future husband or wife, but it might be that he or she hasn't even met that person yet. Social capital develops over time and reveals itself over time.

As a corporate executive, Jason was in a job where people wanted to know him because of his title. He would get calls frequently from people wanting a job, wanting to sell him something, or wanting his organization to sponsor their events. Most of these people weren't trying to network with Jason; they were trying to execute a transaction. But, once in a while, someone took a different approach. One of these people was Jon Duncan. Jon led the executive recruitment team for a large local company. For Jon, Jason was a potential customer in more than one way. While Jon was certainly interested in earning Jason's business, he was also interested in making Jason a part of his network. Jon frequently scheduled social lunches and happy hours where he invited Jason to meet peers from other companies. He would call and ask for help when he needed it and offer help when he could. The thing that made Jon different as a salesperson and connector was that he was always focused on the long-term relationship over the short-term transaction. This has earned Jason's business and loyalty in the years since they've met. The other salespeople have come and gone through the years, but Jon is always a part of Jason's plans.

One key difference between an investment in social capital and a financial investment is that when you invest money, you can't use that money as it's growing. Essentially, you sacrifice the ability to utilize that money elsewhere in return for the potential long-term returns. The relationships that produce social capital work quite differently. Not only do you gain the long-term benefits of a relationship by establishing a connection today, but the relationship can also start paying returns immediately. Every connection you establish has the potential to start creating value immediately through the sharing of information and resources. As this takes place, the relationship grows through the creation of mutual trust and shared experience.

Harnessing Social Gravity

Review the goals you wrote earlier in this chapter. Write some notes about the type of social capital you need to achieve each of these goals.

_____

_____

_____

_____

_____

For each goal, write down what actions you need to take to build the social capital you need to achieve.

_____

_____

_____

_____

_____

Outline a plan for how you will make time to pursue these important, non-urgent activities in your busy calendar.

_____

_____

_____

_____

_____

_____

SOCIAL GRAVITY

CHAPTER 7:

SECOND LAW: BE OPEN TO CONNECTIONS

In order to enter a friend's house, that friend must open the door and invite you inside. Likewise, in order to connect to others, you must first make yourself available to connect by opening the door to your network. This might seem obvious, but consider the following example:

You return from your lunch hour having grabbed a quick sandwich and run some errands. As you look at your phone, you notice that your message light is on, indicating a waiting voicemail. You dial up your first voice mail:

"Hi Joe. My name is Robert White and you don't know me. I was recently having a conversation with your friend Jason, and he thought that the two of us should meet. I'd like to see if I could buy you a coffee sometime in the next couple of weeks to introduce myself and get acquainted. Please return my call at your convenience. My phone number is … . "

What would you do?

☐ Delete the message and pretend like you never got it.

☐ Write down the message and drag your feet returning the call, hoping that Robert doesn't call you again.

☐ Return Robert's phone call and set up a meeting.

Being honest, most people would probably chose either A or B. The first assumption would probably be that Robert wants something from you. He may even want to sell you something. (The horror!) And, human nature makes it hard to reject other human beings, so rather than put yourself through that nightmare, you just avoid meeting Robert all together. You rationalize that it's better for everyone that way.

A few people might choose option C and embrace the opportunity to connect to Robert. It could turn out that Robert shares a common interest of yours, and that's why your friend made the recommendation for you to connect. And, even if Robert does want something from you, that desire is simply serving as a catalyst to make a connection. There are many ways that opportunities to connect will reveal themselves, but you must be open to these opportunities to take full advantage.

The second Law of Social Gravity is Be Open to Connections. As we found from the example above, we are presented with opportunities to connect frequently, and the issue is what to do with those opportunities. Being open to connecting starts first with a mindset that allows you to embrace the opportunities to connect and grow your social capital, and then it expands to taking actions that make you more available for connection. While adopting a mindset to be open to connecting sounds simple on the surface, human nature actually makes this much more difficult than you might expect. We are all prone to making faulty assumptions, relying on stereotypes, and falling victim to cognitive biases, and we often aren't even aware that it's happening. To fully harness the value of social gravity, we must understand our own nature and actively cultivate a mindset of openness to connection with others.

CONNECTED JOE

"Well he is clearly not management material" she whispered to me as the visitor walked away from our booth. We were at a career fair, and the gentleman that had just been visiting with us was dressed casually—very casually. Visiting the career fair in shorts, flip-flops and a T-shirt was not a part of any plan, but on a trip to the grocery store he had bumped into an acquaintance who informed him of this opportunity to network with local recruiters and hiring managers. As someone starting to look for a new opportunity, he decided to stop by.

The recruiter that I was staffing the booth with would ideally be an expert at finding talented people to meet the needs of the organization that we both worked for. Unfortunately, more often than not, recruiters (and the rest of us) seem to be experts at something very different, but much easier, than finding talent: quickly categorizing people. This particular recruiter who disqualified the gentleman because of his dress at the career fair put him in a different category than someone who wanted to attain a management position. And while everyone in the world, including your mother, would recommend you attend a career fair dressed in at least business-casual attire, he was making an unplanned stop at a career fair, not interviewing for a job. And while his attire provided the basis for some assumptions and categorization, it told us nothing definitively about his talent, competency, or ability.

The recruiter was (at least in her mind) removing this person from the talent pool that our organization had access to without having any actual information about his qualifications.

The Connection Mindset

The recruiter in this story was doing something that we all do on a regular basis; she was making a lot of assumptions about a person based on very little actual information. This does not make her a bad person or a lazy person or a bad or lazy recruiter. This makes her human. Each of us is susceptible to the same kind of thinking, regardless of our intentions. Filling in the gaps about other people by making assumptions is a part of the human condition. Assumptions are not about whether someone is a good person or a bad person, and assumptions on their own are neither bad nor good. Sometimes our assumptions are correct, but often they are not. If we are not deliberate about "pushing back" on them, we can easily begin to believe our own assumptions and confuse them with actual facts. This can set us up to make very poor decisions. The recruiter in the story made a decision about whether an individual was "management material" based on nothing but a first impression. Sadly, the consequence of her action was that we may have missed an opportunity to bring someone very talented into our organization. One assumption closed off the opportunity to make a connection that could have been beneficial to the recruiter and the organization.

This very same dynamic can contribute to missing opportunities to build social capital. Every day we are presented with opportunities to connect, and we make assumptions about whether people are worth getting to know or not before knowing anything about them. You don't have to be a serious connecter to have some appreciation for the potential value in meeting or visiting with someone that has celebrity status or is an important business or community leader. For example, most business people would jump at the chance to share a cup of coffee with Bill Gates or Jack Welch because of what we assume could come out of it. At the same time, we may not see a lot of value in setting aside time to visit with a recent college graduate or an old classmate, because we make very different assumptions about the value that could come from those connections. In your organization, would you respond to an invitation to lunch from the CEO the same way you would from the new employee or the person that does administrative work for your team?

Unfortunately, our own human nature works against us in regards to openness. Even if we have the best intentions in the world, things like stereotypes, attribution errors, and cognitive biases all push us toward making assumptions and decisions about people almost instantaneously, and those decisions tend to make us less interested in some people than others. This works as a force in opposition to Social Gravity, so it bears some deeper exploration.

Understanding Human Nature

Stereotypes. Stereotypes are a type of mental schema (or shortcut) that generally take the form of an idea or a characteristic applied to people that we believe belong to a certain social group. We have stereotypes about every social group under the sun. There are stereotypes based on gender, age, race, profession, the part of town you live in, and the car that you drive. Mental labeling or categorizing of others is inescapable, but it can lead you to have more positive or negative feelings toward someone without being based on any real information or experience. If you want to make accurate decisions about people and build authentic relationships, you have to consciously reduce the impact of factors like stereotypes on your decision making about other people.

Even if you do not endorse or agree with stereotypical ideas commonly applied to a particular social group, in the absence of real information, it is very easy to rely on those ideas when making judgments about someone you do not yet know well. We quickly, and often without thinking, categorize people and then apply the stereotypical characteristics to them, whether they be negative or positive attributes.[19] It is not easy to stop yourself from doing this, but you can push back on it by getting in the habit of asking yourself whether you know something about another person or whether you just think you know it. The difference between what you know and what you think you know can be significant.

Attribution errors. In addition to stereotypes, we commonly make judgments called "attribution errors" that contribute to a less than entirely accurate view of the world around us. Attribution errors can cause you to end up with a poorly informed and often skewed understanding of the behavior of people that you interact with. Joe, for instance, struggles with attribution errors almost every day of his life at a four-way stop that he lives near. At the intersection of 52nd and Blondo Streets in Omaha, Nebraska, there is a four-way stop with four stop signs. As we all know, there are rules for four-way stops that we learn in driver's education. So, we assume that everyone knows whose turn it is to go when we are at a four-way stop. Often, when Joe is traveling through this intersection, someone will decide to "budge" and go before it is actually his or her turn. Joe's automatic response to this is to make some profound judgments about the "budger" as a person. He is likely to think that the budger is a bad and outright rude person by nature. He also thinks ridiculous things like "What is what is wrong with this country?" In his younger years, he probably would have even communicated his frustrations to the offending driver with various hand and arm signals, like the famous one-finger salute!

Joe's frustration might be appropriate, but the truth is that he knows nothing about the person who did the budging or the person's circumstances. Perhaps the other driver just learned some terrible news and is distraught. Or perhaps he is rushing his pregnant wife to the hospital to deliver a baby. In the absence of actual context, Joe fills in the gaps with information informed by his emotional response to the budger. Of course, there have been times when Joe has been running late for a meeting or taking his daughter to school and he has budged at that same intersection. Despite being a budger himself, Joe has never considered himself to be "what is wrong with this country." He does not reach any negative conclusions about his own actions, because he knows the actual context. Joe knows why he made the decision to budge. This is one simple example of how you can end up with a skewed view of the behavior of others. You and I might do the exact same thing, but I can still come to the conclusion that you are a bad person because you do it but I am a good person because I do it. Again, you want your interactions and relationships to be based on more fact than fiction, so you have to push back on these tendencies.

Cognitive bias. Cognitive biases, of which there are many, also can twist how you see the world and interpret the behavior of others. Cognitive biases are simply patterns of deviation in judgment that occur in particular circumstances. Said another way, these are tendencies in thinking that are more about quickly delivering answers than collecting and considering evidence. One of the most common examples is confirmation bias. Confirmation bias is our tendency to notice, pay attention to, and remember things that confirm what we think we already know. We are likely to consider people that hold the same beliefs that we do as intelligent. We are likely to watch a brand of television news that supports and confirms the beliefs that we have about political issues.

If you are like most people, you probably think that you have evolved beyond the influence of things like stereotypes and biases. It is easy to think that those things are more likely to guide people that are "uninformed," "uneducated," or "unenlightened." The truth is that these behaviors are about human nature, not education or enlightenment. They impact every single person alive. If you chose to believe that they don't affect you, you are deceiving yourself. And this deception can get in the way of your success in a major way. It is in our nature as humans to judge and categorize everything around us, including other people. Even when you are trying to make yourself available to connections, your brain is constantly making judgments about the people you meet that can prevent you from establishing a meaningful connection with those people. If you determine in the first few seconds of an interaction with another person that he or she is not very professional or interesting, might that change how you approach the interaction going forward? Think about how the recruiter jumped to an immediate decision regarding the potential of one applicant based only on a first impression, without the benefit of even a brief conversation that could have provided a great deal of contradictory information.

Sometimes recruiters and salespeople say it is simply bad business to make assumptions about people or to be influenced by stereotypes. The concept is good, but it denies some of the reality of human nature that our feelings and beliefs about other people are the products of conscious, logical, and deliberate thought. We all make assumptions and we are all influenced by stereotypes, regardless of intentions or business acumen. If you are not able to embrace this, you are not likely to be able to limit its impact.

Cultivate a Beginner's Mind

One of the first American Zen masters, Shunryu Suzuki, often spoke to his students about the concept of having a "beginner's mind," summarized in his famous quote, "In the expert's mind, there are few possibilities; in the beginner's, there are many." Having a beginner's mind serves as a good aspiration as you meet and interact with new people. Your goal should be to put aside what you think you know about other people (assumptions) so that it does not prevent you from what you might learn from them and about them.

This is much harder than it sounds. The more "experience" you get, the more difficult it becomes to have a beginner's mind. Our brains are trained to find patterns that help us more quickly sort through all of the information that comes our way every moment. If you had a great experience in the past with an individual who grew up in rural Tennessee, you may be more likely to assume that everyone from that area would provide the same quality of experience. This is the work of the "expert" mind, with its rules of thumb and categories.

Strive to have a beginner's mind in your interactions with other people, especially those that you do not know very well. Practice these techniques:

Become a student of the people that you meet. Ask a lot of questions. Become a collector of facts about people. The more you know and learn about a wide array of people, the harder it is to fall victim to stereotypes.

Build your listening and observation skills. Pay attention to what people say and do. Make your judgments based on your actual experience rather than unfounded assumptions.

Even with people that you know well, try to appreciate all of the things that you might not know about them, rather than relying on everything that you think you know. Challenge yourself constantly to ensure you know the difference.

Assume positive intentions with everyone you meet. By choosing to actively assume positive intentions, you don't give your mind the opportunity to fill in the gap with a negative assumption or bias (e.g., assume that the budger at the intersection had a good reason to budge or simply didn't see you).

The Power of Diversity

With expertise comes a false sense of certainty. Certainty, which we often associate with confidence, knowledge, and competence, can be very limiting. Often, new and valuable insights come from the most unexpected places and people. Without intention, our human nature will lead us to make assumptions about people that will get in the way of building important relationships that will expand the power of our social capital. As we discussed in the first section of the book, our default approach to networking will often result in personal and professional networks that are populated with people who are very much like us. It is generally easier to relate to, communicate with, and find common ground with people who have similar perspectives, experiences, and world views.

While there is nothing wrong with having relationships with people who are similar to you, your network can be much more robust if diversity is present. So, you should be open to connections and also be intentional about bringing more diversity into your network. And you should look for evidence that you are actually doing these two things. In Achieving Success, Wayne Baker provides the framework for a simple social-network analysis you can use to look for this evidence.

Personal Social Network Analysis:

From time to time, people discuss important matters with other people. Looking back over the past six months, who are the people with whom you discussed matters important to you? (List one to five people.)

_____

_____

_____

_____

_____

Consider the people you communicate with in order to get your work done. Of all the people you have communicated with during the last six months, who has been the most important for getting your work done? (List one to five people.)

_____

_____

_____

_____

_____

Consider an important project or initiative that you are involved in. Consider the people who would be influential for gettig it approved or obtaining the resources you need. Who would you talk to to get the support you need? (List one to five people.)

_____

_____

_____

_____

_____

Who do you socialize with? Socializing includes spending time with people after work hours, visiting one another at home, going to social events, going out for meals, and so on. Over the last six months, who are the main people with whom you have socialized informally? (List one to five people.)

_____

_____

_____

_____

_____

Combine the lists and take some time to analyze the composition of your network. Look especially for the following types of diversity:

- Gender

- Level of formal education

- Race or ethnicity

- Discipline or profession

- Experience living or working abroad

- Political affiliation

- Religious affiliation

This analysis might help you to have some appreciation for the influence of human nature. If you are like most people, you will see limited diversity in your network. Wayne Baker found that more 90 percent of Americans have networks that are composed entirely of the same race or ethnicity.

The fact is that we are drawn to those that we see as being like us, so we find ourselves with social networks populated by those like us (same background, same profession, same age range, etc.). Regardless of what your intentions might be, this is at least partially due to some of the assumptions you make about who you could and should be networking with. Push back on this. Start mixing things up a little and put yourself in different environments and settings so that you start developing relationships with people that will bring new ideas, information, and perspecitves to your personal network. This is the essence of being open to connection. It's not just about time or availability; it's about opening your mind to different people and experiences.

Put Yourself Out There

Now that you have opened your mind to embracing the opportunity to connect, the next step is to take specific actions to make yourself more available to these opportunities to connect. Thanks to the internet, you now have many ways to make yourself more available to those with whom you'd like to connect. As we discovered in Chapter 5, social media provides with a host of powerful tools both for getting in proximity to those who you'd like to meet and also for attracting those people to you. But the internet isn't the only way to make yourself more open and available to connections. Any way you can make it easier for the people with whom you'd most like to connect to find and reach you is an important part of becoming more open to connecting. Here we will talk about a few important steps to get you started.

Return all phone calls and email messages. Depending on the type of work you do, you are going to get solicitations and messages from people you don't know. As we discussed earlier in this chapter, it will be tempting to ignore these requests. Resist that temptation. Take the time to respond. Connections are formed between people. People's situations change throughout their lives. That salesperson leaving you a voicemail today could be your daughter's basketball coach tomorrow. People connect to people, and people are not one dimensional. Nobody fits nicely and neatly into any one category that you might assign them to. Embrace the opportunity to connect, even if you are suspicious of the motive for the call or email. It is important to note that not every connection is going to be a good one. There are people out there who are jerks and who will waste your time. The problem is that you don't know until you meet them. Being open means being open to the jerks in order to find the great and valuable connections. The two go together, and there are a lot less jerks out there than you think.

Use social media. Social media and social networking sites are one of the most powerful things to happen to connecting since the creation of language. Never before has it been easier to find, get introduced to, share information with, and stay in touch with people. However, as we touched on in Chapter 5, the problem with social networking sites is that, if you aren't using them, you can't be found. Since the purpose of this book is not to teach you to use social media (there are many books you can find for that), we will simply give you a couple of critical suggestions on how to use the sites. The most important step is to identify the major sites and establish a robust profile. An effective profile will have the following components:

- Photo. If you met someone briefly, he or she can use your picture to remember who you are and where you met.

- Completed profile. For some sites, this will include your professional information. For others, it might be more related to where you grew up and went to school. All of this information helps others find you, so fill it out.

- Description of yourself. This should help others identify what kinds of connections you might be interested in. If you are looking to network with other skiing enthusiasts, put something about skiing in your description. If you completed the recommended work on your personal brand, this is where you highlight your brand.

Social media by its nature is designed both to be very open and to facilitate connections (hence the word "social"). Once you put your information out there, the requests to connect will start to present themselves. Receive and embrace those opportunities to connect by responding and following up on them when there's an opportunity to expand a relationship further.

Seize opportunities to meet new people. As you become more open to connecting, you will start to recognize opportunities for connection all around you. Any time you are invited to lunch or a social gathering with new people, jump at the opportunity. Every opportunity like this is a chance to make a number of new connections. If you are invited to a networking event, make the time to attend, even if you don't like networking events. If a recruiter calls to recruit you for a job, take the call, even if you are happy in your job. You may need to know a good recruiter in the future, or the recruiter may have a job that would be great for someone else you know. Anytime you are around a new group of people, particularly people you don't know well, it is a great opportunity to cultivate new connections.

CONNECTED JASON

When I first moved to Omaha, I needed to find a new place to get my hair cut. Eventually, I found my way to a salon and a particular stylist named Tanya. Since I keep my hair pretty short, I get my hair cut frequently. This also means that I see the person who cuts my hair pretty regularly. So, over the next five years, Tanya and I became friends. Every three weeks, I'd show up for a haircut and conversation. Then one day, Tanya dropped some terrible news on me. She was moving to Arizona. But, because Tanya knew me so well, she had already chosen me a new stylist at the salon. Her name was Gina. Thankfully, Gina was good at cutting my hair and I liked her, so I began a new relationship with Gina.

About six months after Tanya had moved, I was in getting my hair cut with Gina and she mentioned that Tanya was coming back into town the next weekend. Gina mentioned to me that she and Tanya were heading out for a few adult beverages on Saturday night and that she thought that Tanya would love to see me if I was going to be out. As it turned out, I too had plans to be out that Saturday with a couple of my friends (including the coauthor of this book). Gina and I exchanged cell numbers and agreed to meet up on Saturday night.

And we did. Our two groups came together to share a few drinks. But, this is not where this story ends but where a new story begins. On that fateful Saturday night in Nebraska, I introduced my best friend, Joe, to my hair stylist, Gina. Sparks flew. That initial meeting turned into a few years of making one another crazy enough to decide to get married. And that marriage has resulted in two beautiful children. Since I had a central role in making the Joe/Gina connection, I like to claim some credit for improving the quality of the world by two beautiful children.

As I look back, I could have made the judgment that my hair stylist didn't have any value to my network or that she couldn't add to my social capital. Thankfully, I didn't. I was open to that connection, and it turned into something amazing that I could have never predicted.

Proximity: Your Secret Weapon

As you will recall from Chapter 3, physical proximity is the leading predictor of who we become closest to. This concept has powerful implications if you chose to embrace it. As discussed earlier, if you dissect our closest relationships, you will likely find that most of these relationships occurred by chance with those who happened to be near you at key moments of your life. You didn't choose to be there with those specific people; it just happened.

But think of the potential if you turn the concept of proximity around and begin to use it to put yourself near those with whom you wish to connect. We each had some sense of this from our high school years, when we saw that the basketball team seemed to be friends with one another, as were the members of the band. And we knew if we wanted to break into those particular social circles, we needed to find a way to join the team or the band. There was no substitute for that kind of proximity.

As adults now, proximity plays just as significant a role as it did in high school. If you work in an office environment, you have certainly observed the power of proximity. You've seen that the people who sit near each other in the office seem to also choose to eat lunch together. If you work in a big corporation, you may have worked with someone who has had the opportunity to work in several divisions of the company. Generally, people who have worked in several areas are better connected than others and, because of those connections, tend to be able to make things happen that others can't.

To make proximity work to your advantage, you must begin first by identifying who it is that you most need to connect with. As you reflect on your goals from the first law and your notes from Section 1, you can probably start creating a list of people (either specific people or types of people) who you would most want to connect to. As an example, if you were a freelance graphic designer trying to grow your own business, your list might include partners in advertising agencies, owners of web design firms, and marketing managers within companies. You might research if people who fit these criteria are involved in particular charities or organizations that you can get involved in. By volunteering to work on committees or projects that they are involved in, the proximity of working together with them will likely give way to several connections.

At work, if you have any flexibility as to where your desk is located, chose to locate nearest the people with whom you need the strongest relationships. If this isn't possible, find reasons to be in that area (eat lunch in their break room). Just the act of passing one another in the hall can establish the foundation for a great connection. One of the most extreme (and awesome) applications of proximity we've heard about in our experience came from an area business leader named Doug. He confessed that when he and his wife moved into a new city earlier in his career, he did extensive research of the local neighborhoods to identify where area business leaders and CEOs lived. He then chose to buy a house in the area that would put him in proximity to the most powerful neighbors. This is an extreme example of putting proximity to work for you.

Not everyone has the opportunity or resources to buy a house next to the CEO, but you can use proximity to make choices that lead to better connections. Next time you have the opportunity to move your workspace location at work, advocate for the location that puts you in the best proximity to make meaningful connections.

Harnessing Social Gravity

1. Brainstorm a list of the times in your life over the past several months when you closed yourself off to connections. Note things like calls or email messages you didn't return, the lunch invitations you turned down, the events you chose not to attend, etc. Commit to not let these opportunities pass you by in the future.

_____

_____

_____

_____

_____

_____

2. Revisit your notes from Chapter 5 about the social media tools that would be most relevant for your networking efforts. Create a complete profile on each site. Establish a weekly "new connection" goal for each site (at first, 10 to 20 new connections per week is not unreasonable).

_____

_____

_____

_____

_____

3. Identify at least three ideas for how you can put proximity to work for you in your life. Be specific in listing what you can do and the impact it would have on your social capital.

_____

_____

_____

_____

_____

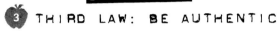

CHAPTER 8:
THIRD LAW: BE AUTHENTIC

Always be authentic. In other words, be who you are. Social capital is built over time. It's built on the strength and consistency of relationships. And relationships form as we create overlap in our shared knowledge and experiences of each other. In order for a relationship to last over time, it must be built on who you are as a person.

> "Your playing small does not serve the world."
>
> –Marianne Williamson

Imagine an awkward high-school boy who is desperately trying to make a good impression with the cute and popular girls in his school. He isn't the greatest athlete, so he can't impress with his athletic abilities. So, in an act of desperation, he tries to put proximity to work for him by signing up for the homecoming committee. Despite the fact that he despises all of the work that this committee will have to do, he signs up because the committee is largely composed of the girls he wants to get close to. How successful do you think he's going to be in the committee? How long will it be before the girls in this group realize his true intentions? And even if he isn't found out, how enjoyable will he find this experience to be? It's not likely that there's a happy ending to this story.

To find a happier ending, this awkward high school boy should have started with thinking about his interests and opportunities. If his family was really involved in their church, maybe getting involved in the church's youth group would have been a better fit. Or maybe, like Jason many years ago, the boy had penchant for performance. Getting involved in the school play or a speech team could be an option. In both cases, this boy is likely to find himself spending time with the girls he so wants to know. But this time, he's there not simply to meet the girls but also to express a part of himself that reflects who he really is. This doesn't guarantee him a girlfriend, but his chances will definitely increase by meeting girls in context of showing his authentic self.

Authenticity in relationships comes from both knowing and acting in alignment with who you are as a person. Each of us is a unique combination of abilities, experiences, passions, talents, beliefs, and interests. What makes connecting to others rewarding is that you will never find another person on the other end of that connection who is exactly like you. Each person brings something new to each relationship. The Third Law of Social Gravity, Be Authentic, requires that you understand the unique value that you bring to your connections and that you act in alignment with that value.

Authenticity Begins With You

In order to authentically connect with others, you must get clear on what you bring to the relationship. This means that the best connectors in the world are those who have a healthy self-awareness. In Chapter 5, we talked about the important of personal brand. Personal brand and the process of developing it both require this kind of self-awareness and refine it. Whether or not you formally develop your personal brand, it's important that you have spent time working on getting clear about what's important to you (what you value) and what makes you unique and remarkable. This is the heart of personal brand. If you aren't sure where you are in the process of becoming self-aware, you aren't alone. Try the following exercise:

The Things I Value Most

_____

_____

_____

_____

The Things That Make Me Remarkable

_____

_____

_____

_____

If this exercise is difficult for you, that's OK. It's difficult for most people. Unless you have already invested in working on self-awareness and your brand, this is likely to be challenging. However, there's no need to be discouraged, because right now is the perfect time to start your journey to self-awareness.

Let's start with getting clear on what's important to you. The most effective way to work through this process is to create your personal manifesto. We have always loved the word "manifesto" because it's a high-impact word that raises powerful reactions in people. The word is formally defined as "a public declaration of intentions, opinions, objectives or motives."[20] We prefer the creation of a manifesto over a more traditional mission or vision statement for two reasons. First, by definition, you must share your manifesto with others in order for it to have meaning. Secondly, there aren't many formal requirements of a manifesto other than the following. A personal manifesto must be:

- **Meaningful to you.** What are you here for? Why do you get up in the morning? What are you trying to accomplish? These are the questions that should be answered in your manifesto.

- **Written down.** If you aren't going to write it down, don't bother. There is power in writing things down. Once it's written, it's real and you've made it real by letting it out of your inner mental workshop.

- **Bold in tone and language.** "Be nice to people" might feel like a great thing to have in your manifesto, but does that language move you? "Blow people away with my kindness and generosity" would be a better choice (if it accurately reflects what you are trying to do). Overly safe statements that are easy to achieve have no place in a manifesto. This is your declaration to the world, so make it count.

- **Shared with others.** By definition, a manifesto is a public declaration. The act of sharing the manifesto with others is powerful because it invokes an underappreciated force to aid you in your personal journey: the power of peer pressure. Once you share the manifesto with others, you know that they will expect to see you living in accordance with the words you've declared. Even if those with whom you share the manifesto never say another word to you about it, you know that they know what you've committed to in your life, and that simple fact will help you stay on the path toward achieving what you declared. We all let peer pressure force us into doing plenty of stupid things; isn't it time to use its power for good?

While we wish we could make this process seem more substantial and complicated, it's really that simple. You just have to sit down and work on it. It doesn't have to be perfect; you simply need to start. And your manifesto is never final, as it should change throughout your life. As your life evolves, so will your manifesto.

CONNECTED JASON

As of the writing of this book, this is my personal manifesto. I share it with you both as an example of a written manifesto and also to model that a manifesto must be shared as if to declare to the world why you are here and what you intend to do.

Jason's Manifesto

- Overwhelm my family with love and support.
- Be a stellar role model for my children.
- Fly my freak flag proudly.
- Make good things happen.
- Learn and grow every day.
- Live courageously.
- Invest generously in my community.
- Be the solution.

The manifesto helps you clarify what you are here for, but self-awareness stretches beyond intentions and values. Kevin and Jackie Frieberg wrote an insightful and energizing book called Boom! 7 Choices for Blowing the Doors off Business-as-Usual that provides a powerful insight into the power of authentic self-awareness. This insight is built on their definition of "congruence." Congruence is defined by the Freibergs as when your individual gifts, talents, and passions equal what needs to be done. We prefer to think of it as an equation:

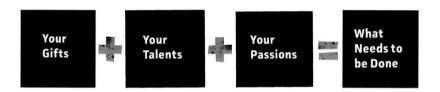

This is a useful concept in many ways. In the next chapter, we will apply this idea of congruence as we examine how to get involved in meaningful activity. For now, the left side of this equation provides powerful guidelines to use as you continue to build our self-awareness. Before you can make any evaluations of congruence to any situation, you must first be clear on your own gifts, talents, and passions.

Gifts and Talents

Each of us has unique gifts and talents. These are the tools you have to add value to a relationship or organization. It's important to think very openly about all of your talents and gifts. Take the time to make a list. Don't judge the value of the skill; just write it down. It could turn out that your expert knowledge of fly fishing could be important to an organization at some point. Use the following guide to help you make your list:

- **Skills.** What are you trained to do? What are you good at? What things do you feel proficient doing? This could range from using PowerPoint to sewing to throwing a football.

- **Knowledge.** On what subjects or topics do you know more than other people? What did you study in school? What books have you read on what topics? Inventory the areas where you bring specific knowledge that is more than what the average person would know. This knowledge can come from your job or from your hobbies and interests.

- **Favorite abilities.** What things do you do that make you feel energized? Everyday, there are things we do that give us energy and things that take our energy away. If you pay close attention, what are you doing each day that makes you feel the most energized or jazzed? Chances are, these are areas in which your natural talents lie.

Passions

Now that you've created your list of gifts and talents, let's turn our attention to your passions. What would you say if asked what you are passionate about? Would you blush? Would you have a ready answer? Passion is defined as any powerful or compelling emotion or feeling such as love or hate. To identify your passions, you need to identify the things you love. Think about the following questions and write out your answers:

- If you had to read a nonfiction book on any topic, what topic would you choose?
- If you suddenly found yourself with an extra week that you could spend any way you wanted to, what would you do?
- When you daydream, what do you think about?
- If you were to win the lottery today, what would you do for the rest of your life to give your days meaning?

As you answer these questions, look for the common themes. Pull these themes out and make a list. These are your passions. Your passion list can include anything from dogs to family to astronomy.

Fly Your Freak Flag

Having equipped yourself with a personal manifesto and an inventory of your gifts, talents, and passions, it's time to consider how much of this value you are revealing to the world through your actions and your relationships with others. Being authentic means that you will stand out from the crowd, as anyone being true to themselves is one of a kind.

Also keep in mind that we are far more dynamic, fluid beings that we probably realize. You are not static and set in stone. Some of us are very different on Monday mornings than we are on Friday afternoons. We are also different in each of our relationships. We bring different parts of our identities to our work relationships than we do to our personal relationships. We bring different parts of our identities to our relationships with our parents than we do with our spouses.

We all make decisions, consciously or otherwise, about what parts of ourselves to share in a given relationship. It is important to have some awareness of this, especially in relation to the fact that one of the most powerful urges we have as human beings is the urge to fit in. We want to fit in, to be accepted, to feel like a part of something larger than ourselves. We are herd animals.[21] This is good in that it pushes us to be social, but the flipside is that conformity is a beast. It is ravenous, insatiable, and it is always at work. It chips away at our edges and our sharp corners, trying to make us just like everyone else. Especially in the workplace, with all the politics, ladders, and career paths to be navigated. People often think that social pressure ceases to be a factor once you graduate from high school, but communities and teams of educated adults are extremely conformist, as well. There is nearly always a whispering in your ear: fit in, don't stand out, and don't draw attention.

Consequently, we each have a tendency to downplay who we are. We have a tendency to not share the unique stuff about us. We share fewer ideas, speak up less, and take up just a little less space. And that is a big part of why authenticity is a fairly rare commodity. It does not seem quite as safe and does not feel quite as comfortable, because it leaves you standing out from the crowd.

Each of us is one of a kind. Truly. Not in a "koombaya, " let's-all-hug kind of way. Scientifically, every single one of us is an original, one of a kind. We are each so much more than what our business cards say about us. We need to be in the habit of sharing more of that other stuff with the world.

As Marianne Williamson says so brilliantly in the quote at the beginning of this chapter, playing small does not serve the world, and it also does not help you build social capital. Ninety-nine percent of who and what you are is invisible and untouchable, and if you want me to understand how valuable my relationship with you is, you have to share more of that stuff with me. You need to share your uniqueness with me. That helps us find common ground, and it helps me remember you. By choosing to be authentic, you provide others with more of the stuff that makes you unique and memorable.

Part of your responsibility as you embrace the connection mindset is to be a little bit less normal and a lot more authentic. It is okay to fit in less and take up a little more space. It's that uniqueness that others will remember and be drawn to. Be who you are, and your authenticity will become the magnetic force at the center of a vibrant network of relationships.

We call this flying you freak flag. Do it now. Do it often. Do it proudly.

Harnessing Social Gravity

1. List your values.

2. Write your manifesto.

3. Write down a list of your talents, gifts, and passions.

4. Make a list of how you can share more of yourself with people around you.

   - How can you be more authentic at work?

   _____

   - How can you be more authentic with your friends?

   _____

   - How can you be more authentic with your family?

   _____

CHAPTER 9

FOURTH LAW: GET INVOLVED IN MEANINGFUL ACTIVITY

In his brilliant book Achieving Success Through Social Capital, Wayne Baker explains that social capital is an outcome that cannot be directly pursued or obtained. In this way, he says that social capital is like happiness. We all want to be happy. But we know that happiness doesn't come in a bottle, and it can't be purchased at any store. Happiness is not something that can be directly pursued. Instead, happiness is an outcome of activities and attitudes. So, when we say we are pursuing happiness, what we mean is that we are pursuing activities and experiences that we expect to make us happy.

What Have You Done for the World Lately?

So, this is a good-news, bad-news situation. If you have always disliked formal networking events, you might be on to something. It turns out that networking for the sake of networking isn't terribly effective, at least not over the long term. Trying to befriend someone simply because you need something specific (such as a sale or getting an introduction) may result in a short-term exchange of value, but it generally has little to do with building social capital. These connections are cosmetic at best and manipulative at worst. Ultimately, this is the reason why events that are designed for the sole purpose of networking often feel a bit awkward or contrived. Unless you are naturally extroverted and you just love meeting people, it can be hard to find common ground on which to authentically connect in these settings.

Social capital, like happiness, is an outcome. It is a byproduct of authentic connections and relationships formed with other people. It is a function of the people that you know and the people that they know. Relationships formed authentically and organically result in the most significant social capital.

And, according to Wayne Baker, one of the most organic sources of valuable relationships is collaboration around meaningful activity. In other words, social capital is more likely to emerge from your interactions with others in the context of shared purpose than it is to emerge from interactions in the context of pure socializing.

CONNECTED JOE AND JASON

Several years ago, Jason and I worked together to create a not-for-profit organization called Next Generation Omaha. The organization had the mission of engaging and giving voice to young professionals living and working in Omaha. Roughly translated, we wanted to help be a driver of positive change in the community and to help make Omaha a cooler place for people to live and work. We were really passionate about this issue and, we were frustrated (bordering on angry) with some of the city leaders at the time. We had talents for bringing people together, for starting dialogue, for communicating ideas, and for inspiring passion in others. So, we set out to make some change.

In our efforts to build and lead this organization, we met and interacted with hundreds of people from across the community. The ironic thing is that we weren't really looking to network. Each of these relationships started from a positive and authentic place of caring about our community and wanting to work together to make progress. We connected with all types of people, including some of the most influential business and political leaders in the city, people who may have been difficult to meet under different circumstances. It turns out that when you call an important civic or business leader and ask for an opportunity to pitch them an idea about how to help their community, many will make time to meet.

These efforts and the network we created contributed in at least small ways to the creation of several young-professional initiatives and efforts that have had lasting impact on the landscape of the city. In fact, our work with Next Generation Omaha led to our involvement in the creation of the Young Professionals Council in Omaha, which has become one of the largest and most successful organizations of its type in the country.

Real relationships were born out of this intersection of people working together because of a shared interest in the future of our community. As a result, our social capital grew enormously. People we met during this time have become close friends, coworkers, business partners, and more. All as a result of our desire to help improve our community.

Meaningful activity is activity that is a true extension of your values. The reason that involvement in meaningful activity is so powerful is that you come together with other people around a common purpose, one that you all share passionately or emotionally. If you join a team to build a house for Habitat for Humanity, you come together with all of the other volunteers on a common level, with a common reason for being there. Regardless of your professional or personal situation, your skills or interests, it is clearly understood when you show up to volunteer that you are there for the purpose of helping build a house that will make a difference in the community. And as you are painting a wall or installing a window with a person who you just met, a conversation might start. This conversation might lead to the exchange of contact information, and thus a connection is born. This connection is built on the foundational knowledge that you came together trying to make a difference in your community. That shared context is a powerful place to form a connection. Being involved in meaningful activity is significant for many reasons, but this is the power of involvement in meaningful activity specific to social capital.

Choose Wisely

It's in the seeking out of meaningful activity that the Freibergs' definition of congruence becomes very useful. As a reminder, they define congruence in this way:

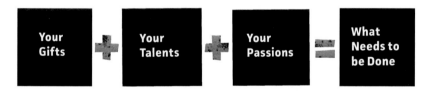

In the previous chapter, you created a list of your gifts, talents, and passions. Now, you can connect those things to something that needs to be done, some meaningful activity. There are many organizations and clubs in every community looking for new members, volunteers, and leaders. Use your list of passions to identify two or three areas you'd like to pursue. Let's say for example that two of your passions are sports and teaching children. If your skills list includes playing sports, you could consider being a youth sports coach through your local parks and recreation department or YMCA. If you do not play sports but are good with managing details, you could volunteer to help organize a youth sports league for the same organizations. If you are unsure, you could pick up the phone and call your local youth sports organization to tell them what you are interested in and what skills you can bring to the table.

At your workplace, there may be committees or projects that need volunteers. These opportunities not only help you build valuable connections that lead to social capital within the organization, but they also show you as a team player who can contribute above and beyond your assigned job. By knowing what you bring to the table, you are likely to find your way to meaningful activity in which you can get involved and make a difference.

Meaningful activity can take many forms. If you are passionate about your work, there are probably a number of professional societies or organizations that you can join and perhaps volunteer to help lead as a part of a committee. If you are more focused on raising a family, there are parent teacher organizations and booster clubs at nearly every school. You may also want to consider a homeowners' association or social club in your community. Even recreation and sports clubs can be meaningful activity if that's where your passion lies (e.g., bicycling or running clubs, volleyball teams, etc.).

Once you start seeking out activities to get involved in, you will find them. There is always more work to be done than there are people to do it, particularly in the realm of volunteerism and community building. Don't assume that because an activity is meaningful that it can't also be strategic and part of your efforts to grow your social capital. As you evaluate where to invest your time and talents, consider which opportunities best align to your connection goals and, more specifically, what opportunities will give you the chance to be in proximity to the people you most want to connect with.

Seeking relationships in a context that is reflective of who you are is a powerful practice for building social capital. No matter where you get involved, you'll build new and important relationships with others that will be built on the foundation of what really matters to you. By seeking out meaningful activity that is both strategic and congruent for you, you will likely form great connections, make a difference, and have a great time while you are doing it.

The Networking Event

You now know that the best way to make connections is through meaningful activity, and you also know that traditional networking events aren't highly effective. But, let's be practical. You will find yourself in traditional networking situations frequently where you don't have the advantage of a common shared purpose to provide a foundation for connection.

It's important to be authentic when doing traditional networking. Regardless of your profession, you probably are in the position where you meet new people. This type of interaction is difficult to master, even for the most outgoing personalities. It's tempting when meeting people to try to be someone else who you think might be more interesting to the other person, to put up some type of front. This is a mistake, and you may miss out on the opportunity to make an authentic connection. Since you now have a good understanding of your own interests and passions, making authentic connections will come much more easily if you follow these simple guidelines.

- **Be open to any connections.** (Remember Law 2.) You never know what kind of value might be hidden behind that next handshake.

- **Be curious.** Ask a lot of questions. If questions don't come naturally for you, memorize a few to get the conversation started. What do you do for a living? What do you do for fun? How long have you lived in town? Did you grow up here?

- **Listen.** Be sincerely interested in people's answers and listen for things you have in common. If you pay attention, you're almost certain to find something you have in common with almost anyone you meet. This common bond becomes the authentic foundation on which to create some overlap and develop that connection.

- **Get contact information.** If you make a good connection, ask for contact information to keep in touch. This can be as simple as saying, "Do you have a business card on you? I'd like to keep in touch." If the person doesn't have a card, ask for an email address.

- **Follow up.** If you ask for contact information, follow up with a short email within a day or two. The email need only include a short note that you enjoyed meeting, a mention of your common interest, and your contact information. This establishes to your new connection that you are sincere and can be counted on to follow up. Plus, the other person now has you contact information so he or she can reach you in the future as well.

Harnessing Social Gravity

1. Research three potential opportunities in which you could get involved in meaningful activity in a congruent way.

_____

_____

2. Identify at least one meaningful activity in which you will commit to getting involved.

_____

_____

3. Write out your personal strategy for meeting new people and turning them into connections. This should include the kinds of questions you will ask to break the ice with a new acquaintance and how you will follow up with that person after the initial meeting.

_____

_____

_____

_____

_____

_____

CHAPTER 10:

 FIFTH LAW: USE KARMA TO TURBOCHARGE YOUR NETWORK

Karma is a concept that comes from the Far East. In Hinduism and Buddhism, karma is the effect of one's actions on the individual's future reincarnations. In short, if you live your life well and morally, you will be rewarded in future lives. Most Western interpretations of karma boil it down to the phrase "what goes around, comes around." Our interpretation of karma is that if you do good for others, good will come back to you. Karma has a powerful application to building social capital.

CONNECTED JASON

In the previous chapter, we described our involvement in an organization called Next Generation Omaha. This led us to eventually become heavily involved with the Greater Omaha Chamber of Commerce in the creation of a new young professionals council (YPC). Through this work, I had the opportunity to volunteer much of my time and energy in efforts that furthered the work of the chamber. When I was asked to help with something, I made time to do it. I was asked to sit on committees, facilitate discussions, and volunteer as an initial member of this new YPC. I invested a lot of personal time in this work because I believed in what we were doing.

A few years later, the YPC hosted a large annual summit event. The event was expected to draw hundreds of young professionals from the area. It was a big deal for the YPC and the chamber. As an aspiring but yet unproven professional speaker, I had submitted a proposal to present a breakout session at this conference, and my proposal had been selected. So, I was eagerly anticipating the opportunity to present for a small group of the conference attendees. Then Mother Nature intervened.

On the evening before the event, a major snowstorm blew through the area, dumping nearly a foot of snow on the city. The event, however, was not canceled. Undeterred by the weather, the young professionals came out in the snow and made it to the event. The snow was not so kind to some of the planned keynote speakers for the conference. As it turned out, the opening keynote speaker for the conference was snowed in several hundred miles away from the conference. This created a dilemma for the conference planners. This dilemma created an opportunity for my karma to go to work for me.

At 8 a.m. that day, my cell phone rang. It was one of the planners of the event, who explained to me that the keynote speaker was not going to make it and asked if I would be able to step in to do my presentation in his place. This might sound horrifying to many people, but as an aspiring speaker, it was incredible opportunity. An hour later, I was on stage in front of hundreds of people making the most of it. All of the good work I'd done over the years came back to me in one amazing opportunity. Karma happens.

Reciprocity

There is actual science behind the idea that if you do good for others, others will do good for you. In his book Influence, Robert Cialdini examines reciprocation as one of his "Weapons of Influence":

> (Reciprocation) is so widespread that after intensive study, sociologists such as Alvin Gouldner can report that there is no human society that does not subscribe to the rule. And within each society it seems pervasive also; it permeates exchanges of every kind. Indeed, it may well be that a developed system of indebtedness flowing from the rule for reciprocation is a unique property of human culture. The noted archaeologist Richard Leakey ascribes the essence of what makes us human to the reciprocity system: "We are human because our ancestors learned to share their food and their skills in an honored network of obligation," he says. Cultural anthropologists Lionel Tiger and Robin Fox view this "web of indebtedness" as a unique adaptive mechanism of human beings, allowing for the division of labor, the exchange of diverse forms of goods, the exchange of different services (making it possible for experts to develop), and the creation of a cluster of independencies that bind individuals together into highly efficient units.[22]

To simplify this idea of reciprocity, it boils down to this: If someone does something for us, we are compelled as human beings to repay them in some way. Reciprocity becomes an important component in the social currency that exists between you and those to whom you are connected. In fact, it is part of what keeps you bound together. You likely have some intuitive appreciation for this when you think about the difference in your response when asked for help by someone that you do not know as compared to being asked for help by someone that has been helpful to you in the past.

Putting Karma to Work

As we have discussed, social capital is the value that lives in the relationships we have with our connections. The value can take many forms, but one of the most significant is goodwill, defined as "the friendly hope that something will succeed." Human nature predisposes us to root for those who have been good to us. Think back in your life to those who have been of help to you along your journey. It's likely that you'd prefer to repay them in some way, but at the very least you wish them the best of luck in all of their endeavors. You wish them to be successful. This is a powerful concept that is at work behind the scenes in your network whether you know it or not. You are more likely to come to the aid of those who have helped you in the past. Because of our innate tendencies towards reciprocation, it is also true that the people you have helped are waiting for the opportunity to repay a favor to you.

It is fairly simple to put karma to work for you in your relationships. Simply put, if you have the opportunity to help someone and you are in a position to do so without causing harm to yourself, do it. Be generous with people. Utilize the gifts and talents you listed earlier to help others. Just by becoming more aware of your gifts and talents, you will speak more specifically about them to your connections. As your connections grow and become more aware of your talents, you will be called on for help. It will be up to you to take advantage of those opportunities.

As a professional in the field of human resources and recruiting, Jason is frequently called on by friends and acquaintances for job advice. This often includes critiquing resumes, recommending best practices for finding jobs, and providing contacts at other companies to network with. To provide this type of help to others is easy for Jason because of his experience, and it costs him nothing to share it with others. Alternatively, this kind of help is of great value to others who may only search for a job a few times in a career. In a short amount of time, Jason can provide help to people that they would have to pay for elsewhere. Regardless of whether his specific advice directly results in a new job for the individual, that person remembers that Jason took the time to help, and most people offer to return him a favor sometime in the future.

If your talent is accounting, you may have friends who ask your help as they look to start up a new business. Or, your neighbor may be on the board of a nonprofit that needs some pro bono help getting its financial statements in order. If your talent is teaching, you might be called on to assist at a school event or to teach a class to your coworkers. Whatever the request, by helping that individual or group, you are generating goodwill within your network. It can be as simple as volunteering to jumpstart a coworker's car or helping your neighbor move some furniture. Each time you do this, you establish more goodwill with people who want to see you be successful. Because it can have such a profound impact, we like to think of karma as the turbocharger for your network of connections.

It's helpful to revisit the concept of investing from the First Law of Social Gravity. Your network of connections will be valuable to you, regardless of how much you leverage karma. But, if you embrace karma, you invest further value in your network. Knowing 50 people is valuable. Knowing 50 people who desire to do you a favor is powerful. Think of your network like a savings account in which you want to build up goodwill. Each time you help a connection, you make a deposit in the account. The more you put in, the more valuable it becomes.

Tips for how to use karma to build social capital:

- Ask every person you meet, "How can I help you?"
- Promote your gifts and talents on your social networking profiles.
- Volunteer your skills to help others every time you have the chance.

- When someone asks for your help and you don't want to do it, do it anyway.
- Surprise people with your generosity.

Harnessing Social Gravity

1. Create a list of ways that you could leverage your talents, gifts, and passion to help others.

_____

_____

_____

_____

_____

2. Reflect on the past several months and identify times when you chose to help others and times when you did not. Think about why you made those decisions and how you might think of those requests differently in the future.

_____

_____

_____

_____

_____

_____

_____

_____

_____

SOCIAL GRAVITY

CHAPTER 11:

 SIXTH LAW: STAY IN TOUCH

I grew up on a farm in Northwest Iowa, and my mom has always had a serious garden. While I have always loved the fruits and vegetables that come out of my mother's garden, I have never been crazy about the actual work of gardening. That may be the primary reason that my wife and I today have a quite small garden.

There is no cheating in gardening, no shortcut. It is one of those things in which you have to proactively and consistently invest if you want the benefit of the end result. If you want your plants to do well, you have to pull weeds and consistently water the garden. If you want good plants to weed and water, you have to plant in the spring at just the right time. If you want to have decent soil to plant your seeds in, you have to prepare it through tilling and other labor. If you decide to skip any one of these steps or take some shortcuts along the way, it will diminish what you have to enjoy at the end of the summer when it's time to harvest.

Your network works very much the same way. You may not need anything from your connections today. There may not be anything of obvious value coming to you from your network right now, but you must actively care for and grow your network every day so that it can deliver a great "harvest" for you in the future.

Growing your social capital is like growing a garden. If you don't plant the seeds, there's nothing to grow. If you plant the seeds , but don't tend to them after planting, the chance that they will grow up to bear fruit (or vegetables!) is very slim. A successful garden requires work and constant attention. Building and developing social capital works the same way. Making connections (planting the seeds) is only part of the equation for establishing the relationships that lead to valuable social capital. In order for connections to become truly valuable, you must stay in touch (tending the garden).

Historically, salespeople have stood out as a group of people who have mastered the art of staying in touch to develop their networks. After all, their livelihood depends on building relationships with people who will trust them enough to buy something from them. Since it is part of their job, salespeople can take the time to make a call to a prospect every month or two to keep in touch. They send Christmas and birthday cards with personal notes to each of their customers and prospects. It takes a significant investment of time to do these things, so others who are not involved in a career in sales rarely make the time to do these same things to cultivate their networks.

Successful salespeople are good at making this investment in keeping in touch because they understand human nature. As humans, we are drawn toward comfort and away from risk due to our core need to survive. One way we avoid risk is by gravitating toward things and people who we know. The less we know about a person, the more risk we naturally assume. When planning to make a large purchasing decision like a house or a major software system at work, we feel like we can limit the risk by purchasing from someone we "know." Generally, the people we would say we know are not only people who we have met in the past but also people who we have seen recently and who seem to have some interest in us. Salespeople who do this well feel almost like your friends because they've made an investment in developing a relationship with you. They understand the importance of the overlap that was discussed in Chapter 2, and they invest in that overlap. Who wouldn't want to buy something from their friend?

It's All in the Approach

We can learn from those who make their living in sales. When they make connections, they take an intentional approach to growing those relationships. A major component in how they develop those relationships is how they keep in touch with each connection (or prospect). Here we share some of the most effective considerations for keeping in touch with your connections.

Appropriate. Choosing the right way to follow up with a connection depends on the specific person. Depending on the age and preference of your new connection, the approach you use to keep in touch may vary widely. There are people within every network who still haven't embraced email, much less social networks. If you email a follow-up note to such a person, your efforts will be wasted. Instead, you may want to drop them a phone call after a few weeks or even send a handwritten thank-you note with your business card. On the other hand, if you took that same approach with a tech-savvy young professional, you may appear old-school and out of touch. When making a connection, it's best to ask how that person prefers to keep in touch and then use that as your guide.

Consistent. The goal of staying in touch with your connections is to grow the relationships. In essence, you want to be top of mind for your connections. The goal is to be someone they think of first if asked "Do you know someone who … ." Being top of mind has always been the goal of advertisers, and they know that it can only be achieved through repeated exposure to their message or brand.[23] This same concept needs to be applied to your efforts to grow relationships with your connections. This means that you need to keep in some sort of regular and consistent contact with your connections. Depending on the contact, this will also vary. For some contacts, you might want to touch base once a month if that is appropriate for both of you. For others, a holiday card or a note on Facebook once per year might do the trick. Regardless of frequency, you have to consistently reach out to every one of your connections.

Relevant. The very best salespeople and networkers make you feel as though they are invested in you. They add value to your relationship by proactively providing you with information and resources that you care about. They do this by asking questions of their connections over time and keeping notes of what they learn. If you spent much time with the authors, you'd probably find out that we are both active bicyclists. This piece of information might allow you to create unexpected value for us in the future by sharing information about new bike tours or products. Once you learn information about your connections, the next step is to use that information to create value for them. This can be as simple as asking a connection about their kids when you see them or as involved as introducing members of your network to one another who share common interests.

The Technology Effect

Today, keeping in touch is much easier than it was in the past. With the advent of email, the time-consuming process of sending personalized notes became as fast and easy as typing a few words and clicking send. In addition to email, social media sites like LinkedIn and Facebook have given us more and easier ways of staying in touch. Today, if I change jobs and want to notify my connections of where to find me in the future, I can email my entire address book my new information. Additionally, if I update my LinkedIn profile, it will post a note for my connections to let them know that I've moved. And this all happens in the blink of an eye.

As social networking sites have grown in popularity, so has the opportunity to connect with others. After meeting someone, it's simple to send a LinkedIn request and have it accepted. Once that occurs, this connection becomes part of your network. Due to the ease of these connections through LinkedIn, Facebook, and other sites, it's not uncommon to quickly find yourself with hundreds, if not thousands, of connections to manage. Since many of us struggle to keep up with our day-to-day responsibilities the way it is, how can we possibly keep up with all of these connections? Is it even possible?

In Chapter 3, we discussed Dunbar's number, which says that a person can only manage approximately 150 active relationships at any given moment. If this is true, what does this mean if you have 600 connections on LinkedIn and 400 friends on Facebook? Clearly, you can't maintain close relationships will these hundreds of contacts. However, social media is a powerful new tool that gives you the ability to stay connected to large numbers of people so that you know where to find them when you need them, even if you haven't actively maintained a more substantial relationship with them in the meantime. Social media keeps the connection intact. It might help to think of your online network in terms of active and latent connections.

- **Active connections** are the up to 150 connections with whom you are actively engaged in relationship building. These connections are those who you'd keep notes on and consistently follow up with. There is a fair amount of overlap in these relationships. It's likely that you have a compelling reason to stay in touch with this group of people personally or professionally.

- **Latent connections** are in no way less important than your active connections, but they are simply connections that you are not as actively engaged with currently. Your online latent connections are those who we've referred to as acquaintances or "weak ties." This group might include childhood friends or classmates, past coworkers, or old neighbors. They are probably all people who you have had good intentions to stay in touch with but, due to life changes or changes in proximity, aren't within your active circle today. The brilliance of social media tools is that you can maintain a connection with each of these people and even keep them up to date with what's happening in your life by updating your profile. The advantage is that, someday, when you might need to make them an active connection again, you can find them easily and re-ignite your connection.

Leveraging Technology

To this point in this chapter, we've focused on a very individualized approach to staying in touch with your connections. But we are realists and we know that it's simply not practical to individually manage each of your active connections, whether you have 20 or 150. Staying in touch means employing a variety of techniques, including those that allow you to reach several people with one action.

Being involved in meaningful activity means that you will probably interact with a number of people and organizations within your community. In our experience, that means that you will hear about opportunities frequently, such as fun events, volunteer opportunities, or even jobs at different companies or nonprofits. One easy way to stay in touch with your contacts is to create an informal email list to which you send out these opportunities when you hear about them. Within most email programs is the feature to create a distribution list of several email addresses, allowing you to email the entire list with one click. Create your list of contacts with whom you'd like to keep in touch. Remember that you'll need to add new contacts as you meet them. When you hear of a great opportunity or event that you think many of your contacts would find interesting, prepare a short email to send out to your list. Below are a few guidelines to follow:

- Send out emails on opportunities that are not widely known about already. Choose to email information that will position you as an "insider" source of information for your contacts that they might not hear about elsewhere. If you don't have this kind of information, you aren't involved in enough meaningful activity or you haven't built enough contacts. Either way, you can correct that situation.

- When sending on information from an email sent to you, clean up the email so that only the important information is included. Always put a personal note at the top of your email that describes why you are forwarding the information out.

- Don't simply forward on an email to your list without any personal comment. Forwards can be annoying and you lose the value of the personal touch that should be included when you reach out to your contacts.

- Use the blind carbon copy (BCC) line when you select the distribution list to ensure that the email addresses of your contacts are protected. Opportunistic people will harvest email addresses from forwarded emails. If this happens to your list, you may lose credibility with your contacts. Don't risk it.

- Try to send out an email to everyone on your list at least once per year, but no more than once per month.

- Keep your emails short and to the point. Include some well wishes in the email (e.g., "I hope that this email finds you well") and encourage them to contact you if you can do anything for them.

This method may sound a bit impersonal, but it can be highly effective. By sending an email, you ensure that they see your name and email address at least once per year, preferably more. While they may not be interested in the information you send, they can delete the email and still be thankful that you thought to send it to them. The email serves its purpose by letting your contacts know that you are thinking about them and ensuring that they are thinking about you. This takes a little effort, but not nearly the effort of sending personal handwritten notes, and it is highly effective for staying in touch with your contacts.

In addition to email, there are many other ways to keep in touch with your contacts.

Social networking sites. Websites like LinkedIn, Facebook, and Plaxo have provided us with great resources and tools for staying connected and keeping in touch with our connections. While these sites may seem a bit overwhelming at first, once you spend a little time getting to know them, you'll find that you can work with them easily. It is important to think of these sites as your portal to your connections. It's likely that you will need to establish profiles on several sites.

When you use these sites, complete a full profile with your work history, community involvement, professional affiliations, and even colleges and universities you attended. This allows your connections to learn more about you and possibly even find more things that you have in common. As we discussed in Chapter 5, we also recommend posting a picture with your profile. Many people remember faces rather than names. Including your picture makes it easier for your newer connections to remember your interaction.

When you meet someone who you'd like to stay connected with, inquire with them about whether they use any of these sites. If they use LinkedIn, follow up with an invitation to connect. When sending out an invitation to connect, put a personal note in the invitation. Many people out there send invitations to people they may not even know. Take the extra few seconds to include a note about who you are and why you are asking them to connect. It matters.

Phone calls. In the age of email, text messaging, and instant messenger, the telephone has become a nearly forgotten tool. For people who are important to stay in closer touch with (e.g., someone who can help you in your career field), it's a good idea to make a phone call to them on occasion. The frequency of the calls will vary based on the contact. The call can be as simple as this: "Hi John, this is Jason Lauritsen. We haven't talked in a while, so I thought I'd check in to see how life has been treating you. What's new on your end?" The personal touch of a phone call in addition to your emails is a nice touch for connections that are more important.

The written note. If the telephone has been forgotten, the handwritten personal note is an absolute relic. But it still works, and it works well. Handwritten notes stick out because they are rare and because we know that they take a bit more time and effort than "poking" someone on Facebook or firing off a quick text message. Keep a list of people to send notes to at the end or beginning of the year, or try to send one or two personal notes per week.

Breakfast and lunch. While all of the suggestions above are great ways to stay in touch with your connections, there is still no substitute for one-on-one face time. Over the years, we have each individually spent our breakfasts and lunches meeting with our current or new connections. If you spend each day eating lunch at your desk, you are wasting an hour of time that could be invested in your future. Granted, eating out every breakfast and lunch can be expensive. So, start with one lunch per week. Invite someone you want to strengthen your connection with to go to lunch with you. You will be surprised how many people will take you up on your offer. The funny thing is that the content of your discussion at lunch isn't terribly important. Come prepared with questions and curiousity. You'll discover additional interests and passions you share with that contact that will strengthen your connection. Over time, you'll feel that your network is growing and becoming stronger. The lunch is an investment in your network and yourself that is well worth making.

Referrals. Another great way to stay in touch with your connections is by sending them referrals. This may not work for everyone, but it is a good strategy for the right people. As you get to know people, ask them how you can help them. Business owners will likely ask you to send them potential customers or help them get the word out about their products or services. Corporate managers might ask you to be on the lookout for good talent whom you could send their way. Some may even ask you to let them know if you see any good movies or read any good books. You never know how you can help someone until you ask. Once people share with you how you can help them, try to make referrals to them any time you have the opportunity to do so. It's a way to help them and also ensure that they know that you are thinking of them. This also puts the dynamics of reciprocity into play.

These are a few proven ways of staying in touch with your connections. You may need to experiment to discover what works best for you. And remember, not all connections are created equal. Remember the gardening example and make sure that you invest your time and energy in a way that is going to deliver for you the harvest that you desire.

Harnessing Social Gravity

Write out a personal strategy for keeping in touch with your network of connections. This should include the following:

- Who is most important in your network? Identify appropriate, consistent, and relevant approaches for keeping in touch with each of these individuals.

- How can you keep in touch with your latent connections online? Do you post updates to your social media sites? Do you send out emails?

- What kind of rare or unique information can you share periodically with your network as a way of staying visible? If you can't think of anything, consider getting involved in more meaningful activities in your community.

_____

_____

_____

_____

_____

_____

_____

_____

_____

SOCIAL GRAVITY

CHAPTER 12:

IT'S YOUR TIME

It is almost time for us to go our separate ways. We hope that you will now be able to make better decisions and take more well-informed actions regarding social capital. We hope that you know that this matters greatly. And we hope that you will act accordingly.

> "We are called to be architects of the future, not its victims."
>
> — Buckminster Fuller

We have just revealed to you the Six Laws of Social Gravity. These laws, if applied appropriately, have the power to transform your life. Let's recap the laws.

 First Law: Invest in Connecting. Building a powerful network requires significant effort. Knowing your goals, understanding the power of compounding, and taking the long-term approach will lead to more intentional actions for growing your social capital.

 Second Law: Be Open to Connections. In order to make connections, you have to first open yourself up to connections. This starts with cultivating an open mindset and then taking actions to become more easily available to connection opportunities.

 Third Law: Be Authentic. Great connections happen best when freak flags are on display. To authentically connect with others, first you must know yourself and embrace who you are and where you are going.

4 **Fourth Law: Get Involved in Meaningful Activity.** Social capital is an outcome of your involvement in meaningful activity. Getting involved in things that connect to your passions and interests is the best way to cultivate a network with value.

5 **Fifth Law: Use Karma as a Turbocharger.** The best way to turbocharge your network is to freely give your resources and time to your connections. This investment in your network results in a reciprocal effect that exponentially increases your social capital.

6 **Sixth Law: Stay In Touch.** A network is like a garden; to reap a great harvest requires consistent, purposeful work. Making a connection is simply planting the seed of a potential relationship. It won't grow unless you follow up and create overlap over time.

These six laws will unlock the power of social gravity to you. If you seriously invest in living these laws, you will be rewarded with the power to pursue your success. We all define success differently. Some of us are very focused on achieving specific professional goals, such as working for a specific company or getting promoted to a specific job. Some of us have non-work-related goals that we want to accomplish, such as climbing Mt. Everest, getting poetry published, or running a marathon. Some of us focus on happiness, balance, or relationships with friends and family as measures of success. Regardless of how you define success and regardless of what you aspire to, mastering the Laws of Social Gravity can help you make it happen.

And regardless of who you are or where you come from, you can have more social capital tomorrow than you have today if you choose to act now. It is on you and you alone. You do not need a budget, degree, title, or certification. You don't even need to apply for acceptance or get anybody's permission. You just do it. You just do the first right thing. We do not know how this will play out for you, but we do know how it starts. It starts with you putting one foot forward.

Maybe you have known for some time what you want from life. Maybe reading this book prompted some of your first real thinking about that. Knowing is important, but once you have that figured out, action becomes all that matters.

Action becomes the only thing.

Here's the catch. Action requires that you take some risk. Nothing we've presented in this book is particularly hard to do. It's all pretty straightforward, simple stuff to do. But, if you haven't been living according to the laws already, it's likely that some of them sound a bit intimidating. At the very least, you are going to have to get out of your comfort zone and take some risks.

- Will you risk putting yourself out there in social media (picture, description, and the whole works)?
- Will you risk opening yourself up to all types of new connections, even though a few of them might turn out to be jerks?
- Will you risk taking the time to understand your interests and passions?
- Will you risk flying your freak flag by showing your interests, passions, and dreams to others?
- Will you risk getting involved in a group where you don't know anybody?

Say yes. Take the risks. The greatest and most meaningful rewards are not attainable without risks. Start out with some small risks. You'll find that the risks pay off. Then, you'll start taking bigger risks. You'll start putting yourself out there more. Nothing in this book requires you to be an extrovert or to have any special talents with people. You just have to be willing to take a few risks that allow the forces of social gravity to attract tremendous opportunity to you.

What will you do? You likely have some ideas. You have thought of doing some of the things that we have mentioned or tweaking them slightly to better work in your world. Whether you have already generated some ideas or not, the time has come to make some specific commitments so that you can immediately begin putting the ideas in this book to work. We are asking you to commit to doing three specific things in next ten days.

Action, even small simple action is a powerful antidote to procrastination, doubt, fear, and uncertainty. The most important thing that you can do right now is to make some simple commitments and then get on with carrying them out. Spend some time online, commit to one breakfast each month, pick up the telephone and reach out to someone, make time on your calendar for connecting and re-connecting, or write a personal note. Small steps consistently taken will have a positive impact on your social capital.

When things of substance collide, they often throw sparks. Now is your time to throw sparks. Go create intersections. Seek out new people, people that are different from you, people that are different from the other people that you know, and crash into them. Do that consistently and you will find yourself afloat in an ocean of expertise, ideas, perspectives, and experiences. You will find yourself benefitting from social gravity, making it easier for the good stuff in the world to find you.

Go light your world on fire.

WHAT YOU WILL DO	WHEN YOU WILL DO IT

Appendix

APPENDIX 1:
SURVEY QUESTIONS

In September 2010, in conjunction with Quantum Workplace, we conducted a survey that consisted of a total of nine questions that were designed to gather employee opinions about the importance of networks and relationships in the workplace, particularly as it relates to getting ahead. We also designed some questions to probe how individuals feel about promotional decisions that are made based on relationships. Our survey sample included 979 responses from employees at a wide range of employers in seven major U.S. cities. Below are the questions that were included in that survey.

Question set:

1. An employee's relationships at work should be considered in decisions about advancement.
   ☐ TRUE ☐ FALSE

2. It is important to have a strong network of relationships at work.
   ☐ TRUE ☐ FALSE

3. Knowing the right people is critical to getting promoted in my organization.
   ☐ TRUE ☐ FALSE

4. The quality of an employee's work relationships is a good indicator of the individual's work performance.
   ☐ TRUE ☐ FALSE

5. An employee's skill at networking inside the organization is valuable for both the employee and the organization.
   ☐ TRUE ☐ FALSE

6. It is unfair when someone gets promoted at work because of who they know.

☐ TRUE ☐ FALSE

7. What ONE factor does your organization evaluate MOST when determining whom to promote:

☐ Leadership potential

☐ Success at individual goals

☐ Strength of relationship between candidate and decision maker

☐ Senior executive's "gut instinct"

☐ Formal education and credentials

8. What ONE factor should your organization evaluate MOST when determining whom to promote:

☐ Leadership potential

☐ Success at individual goals

☐ Strength of relationship between candidate and decision maker

☐ Senior executive's "gut instinct"

☐ Formal education and credentials

9. Please respond to the following cliché: "Who you know is more important than what you know." (e.g., Do you agree? If so, is it fair?)

_____

_____

_____

_____

_____

APPENDIX 2:
SUGGESTED READING

If you are like us, once you get started thinking about the power of networking, you are going to want to read more. So, we've prepared for you a list of the best books related to the creation of social capital.

How to Win Friends and Influence People by Dale Carnegie

The Tipping Point by Malcolm Gladwell

Achieving Success Through Social Capital by Wayne Baker

Linked by Albert-Laszio Barabasi

Nexus by Mark Buchanan

Emergence by Steven Johnson

The Wisdom of Crowds by James Surowiecki

Six Degrees by Duncan Watts

Dig Your Well Before You're Thirsty by Harvey Mackay

Guerrilla Networking by Jay Conrad Levinson and Monroe Mann

Never Eat Alone by Keith Ferrazzi and Tahl Raz

The Hidden Power of Social Networks by Rob Cross and Andrew Parker

REFERENCES

i   Allison Aubrey, "Happiness: It Really Is Contagious," *NPR*, December 5, 2008 (http://www.npr.org/templates/story/story.php?storyId=97831171).

ii   Sheldon Cohen, Ph.D., et al, "Social Ties and Susceptibility to the Common Cold," *The Journal of the American Medical Association*, 1997, Vol. 277(24), 1940-1944.

iii   Pierre Bourdieu, "Ökonomisches Kapital, kulturelles Kapital, soziales Kapital," *Soziale Ungleichheiten*, 249

iv   Carmen Sirianni and Lewis Friedland, "Social Capital," *Civic Practices Network* (http://www.cpn.org/tools/dictionary/capital.html)v Robert Putnam, "The Prosperous Community: Social Capital and Public Life," The American Prospect, Spring 1993, 35-42.

vi   Landon Thomas, Jr., "A $31 Billion Gift Between Friends," *The New York Times*, June 27, 2006.

vii   Donn Byrne and John A. Buehler, "A note on the influence of propinquity upon acquaintanceships," *The Journal of Abnormal and Social Psychology*, 1955, Vol 51(1), 147-148.

viii   Mitja Back, Stefan Schmukle, and Boris Egloff, "Becoming friends by chance," *Psychological Science*, 2008, Vol. 19(5), 439-440.

ix   Leon Festinger, Stanley Schachter, and Kurt Back, Social Pressures in Informal Groups (Stanford University Press, 1950).

x   Charlene Li, Chriss Charron, and Amy Dash, "The Career Networks," Forrester Research, 2000.

xi   Wikipedia, Dunbar's number, http://en.wikipedia.org/wiki/Dunbar%27s_number (December 28, 2011).

xii   Jeffrey Pfeffer, Managing with Power: Politics and Influence in Organizations (Harvard Business School Press, 1992).

xiii   PBworks, The Real Definition of Personal Branding, http://personalbrandingwiki.pbworks.com/FrontPage (December 28, 2011).

xiv   Wikipedia, Warren Buffet, http://en.wikipedia.org/wiki/Warren_Buffett, (December 29, 2011).

xv   The Motley Fool, Why Should I Invest? http://www.fool.com/investing/beginning/why-should-i-invest.aspx (December 29, 2011).

xvi   Investopedia, Compounding, http://www.investopedia.com/terms/c/compounding.asp (December 29, 2011).

xvii   The Motley Fool, Why Should I Invest? http://www.fool.com/investing/beginning/why-should-i-invest.aspx (December 29, 2011).

xviii   Stephen Covey, A. Roger Merrill, and Rebecca R. Merrill, First Things First (Simon & Schuster, 1994).

xix   PsyBlog, Stereotypes: Why We Act Without Thinking, http://www.spring.org.uk/20 /01/stereotypes-why-we-act-without-thinking.php (December 28, 2011).

xx   Dictionary.com, http://dictionary.reference.com/browse/manifesto (December 28, 2011).

xxi   Giuseppe Spezzano, "How The Need to Fit In Changes Our Behaviour," Family Anatomy, November 2, 2009 (http://www.psychologytoday.com/blog/plus2sd/200809/the-stupidity-crowds)

xxii   Robert B. Cialdini, Ph.D., Influence: The Psychology of Persuasion (Harper Business, 2006), 18.

xxiii   Wikipedia, Top of mind awareness, http://en.wikipedia.org/wiki/Top_of_mind_awareness (December 28, 2011).